Google Sketch for Interior Design and Space Planning

GW01417840

Training Course 4

How to communicate your ideas in a convincing way

2nd Edition

Adriana Granados

2011

About the Author

Adriana Granados has a degree in architecture from the University of Buenos Aires, Argentina; an interior design degree awarded by the Universidad Popular de Belgrano, Buenos Aires, Argentina; and completed doctoral studies at the Universidad Politecnica de Catalunya, in Barcelona, Spain. For several years she was the Latin American support for different software programs related to architecture and interior design. She worked as project manager being in charge of quality control in the drawing area of an outsourcing company. She trained for years hundreds of people in the use of different architecture software. She has taught several courses at college level on the use of SketchUp applied to interior design.

Acknowledgement

Thank you to Michael Dugas and Jo Dawson for helping me prepare this manual. Michael drew on his experience in renovation and his studies in the Interior Design program at Salem College to help me with accuracy and accessibility in both the text and the illustrations. Jo, a longtime newspaper copy editor aware that English is not my mother language, helped me present my ideas and instructions clearly and succinctly.

Preface

Google SketchUp® brings together several important features for people who want to venture into the use of design software. It offers a short learning curve, gratifying results right away, low cost of investment in training and in software, and an open platform that provides libraries of all types. Much has been written for using Google SketchUp® in the building shell and its relationship to the environment or the site. Less help has been provided to interior designers who work every day with materials, textures, lights and colors. Students need to know the available tools and how they can apply them in specific cases to a particular discipline. Fundamental concepts, ideas on how to create objects and interior spaces, tips and practical exercises are what this book offers. Rather than endless lines of explanatory text this hands-on book is a compendium of practical exercises that lead students to learn SketchUp from the perspective of the interior designer.

This book focuses on the fundamentals for the interior design field and promotes independent study. It offers four separate courses progressing in complexity. They can be read as one source or be consulted separately for those who already have experience with Google SketchUp®. At the end of every course you will find practical exercises that will broaden your experience in the acquired knowledge. These resources enable students to think about how the knowledge can be applied to any situation. On-line videos reinforce the concepts.

At the end of the four courses you will be able to express your ideas to others in a more efficient and attractive way. Illustrating the "feel and look" of a space will allow others to understand what you have in mind and will help you in your career success.

Training Course 1. Developing Basic Skills

If you are new in the use of SketchUp, going through the basic course exercises will allow you to draw, edit and manipulate various elements. This course may be applied to any discipline, but all exercises are designed especially for interior designers, stage designers, and space planning focusing on the tools required to use SketchUp in those fields. With the acquired information students should be able to evaluate the limitations and capabilities of Google SketchUp® and decide whether if it is suitable for their goals.

Training Course 2. Acquiring Intermediate Skills

Learn how to stay organized in SketchUp by using groups, components and layers. Learn how to control your model through the Outliner and access to the 3D Warehouse.

Training Course 3. Materials and textures, the key for interior design

Learn to apply materials, textures, and use pictures and components. Create new materials from any picture or swatch that you might have. You will learn to create your own libraries of materials and textures, and to modify colors and scales. Real word textures will be used for finishing, carpets, upholstery and curtains.

Training Course 4. How to communicate your ideas in a convincing way

Working with SketchUp interior models is completely different from creating models that can be seen only from the outside. You will learn how to show interior spaces by using various styles and sections, and by bringing in shadows and lighting. You will learn how to use scenes and, animations, export images, print perspectives and drawings in scale, export files to other programs, and import Autocad® files.

Table of Contents

Training Course 4. Communicating and sharing your ideas in a convincing way

Other available training courses

Training Course 1. Developing Basic Skills

1.   **How to start using SketchUp**
    1.1 Tour and tools overview

2.   **How to begin to draw in 2 dimensions**
    2.1   Drawing a single straight line
    2.2   Inference
        2.2.1   Inference Cues
        2.2.2   Linear Inference
        2.2.3   Point Inference
    2.3   Drawing a rectangle with single straight line
    2.4   Using the Erasing Tool
    2.5   Using the Undo and Redo Tools
    2.6   Selecting one element and various elements at the same time
        2.6.1   Adding and subtracting from a selection set
        2.6.2   Adding to the selection set

Training Course 2. Acquiring Intermediate Skills

Practice Chapter 5

Training Course 3. Materials and textures, the key for interior design

Practice Chapter 6

During this training course you will need exercises developed in previous courses as well some other resources. Send an email to sketchup-interior-design@nextcad.net to obtain an access key to download the files.

Chapter 7. How to work in interior spaces and present your work in different styles.

Objectives

When you have completed this chapter you will be able to:

- Apply different styles to your 3D model.
- Use the following commands: Styles, Pre-defined Styles, Edit Styles, Style Settings.

7.1 Styles Browser

When you open a new file in SketchUp your can choose a template by clicking on the **Choose Template** button. However, once you are inside the program you can select a different style. The Styles Browser contains options used to alter the ways your model and the drawing area are rendered (edge types, face settings, background settings, watermarks, and modeling settings). The Styles Browser is activated from the **Window** menu/**Styles**.

7.2 Select tab. Pre-defined Styles

1. Open Tut_6.15 file or open your Components window, type "Tut_6.15 by agra", download it into your file and explode it.
2. Click on **Window** menu / **Styles.**
3. Select **Default Styles** in the drop-down menu.
4. Select any thumbnail on the **Select** tab.
5. Click on different options to see several results.
6. Change the Default Styles folder to **Assorted Styles**. Select other thumbnails.

(2)   (6)

7. Click on the **In Model** 🏠 button. The shown collections will be those that you chose in previous steps. To clear out the folder click on the **Details** button 🗗 and **Purge Unused**.
8. Select again the **Default Styles** collection / **Engineering style**.

7.3 Edit tab

1. Continue with the same file and style.
2. Click on the **Edit** tab. The Edit tab contains five separate panels:
   - Edge Settings
   - Face Settings
   - Background Settings
   - Watermark Settings

- Modeling Settings

7.3.1 Edge Settings

1. Click on the **Edge** button and change setting as shown below.

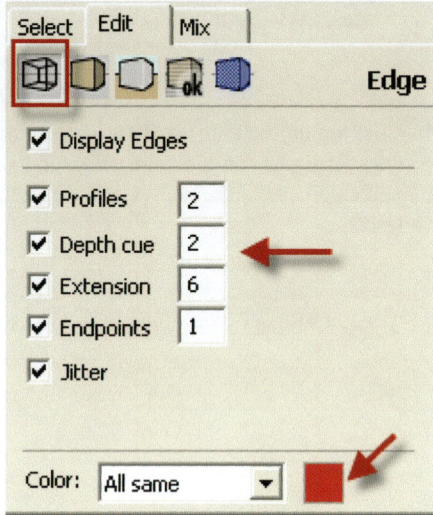

(2)

2. Click on the **Update Style** button. The copy of the style in the **In Model** styles is updated with your changes. If you do not update your style when you switch to another style, the unsaved changes will not be saved.

3. Type a name in the 'File name' field and click the **Create a New style** button. The file is saved. Refer to the Open or create a collection context-menu to retrieve this style for use in other SketchUp files.

4. Open **View** menu/**Edge Style**. Uncheck all the options. Only the faces and textures will be visible (the Shaded with Textures should be checked on the Face Style menu).

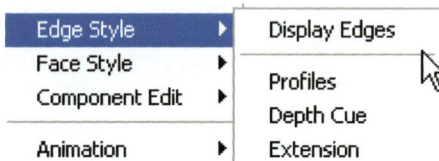

(4)

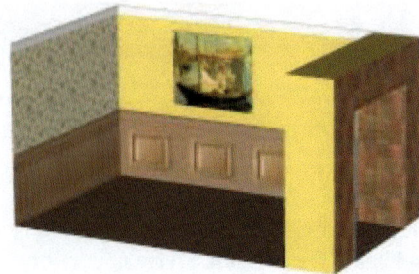

One way of simulating a photorealistic rendering style is to color edges by material. This resource plus applying shadows to your model can change dramatically the way your model looks.

1. Open **View** menu / **Edge Style** / check **Display Edges**.
2. Select with a crossing window from left to right, faces and edges of the left crown molding.

3. Sample the crown molding material with the **Paint Bucket** 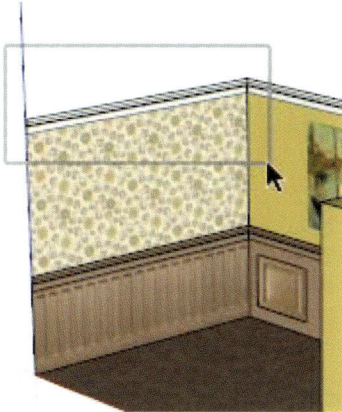 tool + **Alt** key.
4. Release the **Alt** key. Click on the same selected elements to reapply the white color to the edges.

5. Choose the **Select** 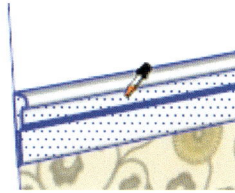 tool to finish painting.

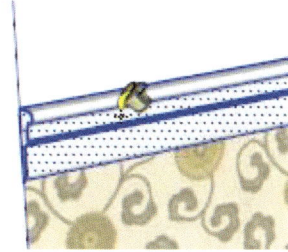

| (2) | (3) | (4) |

6. Open the **Styles** window / **Edit** tab.

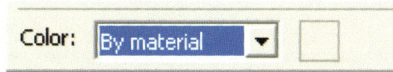

Color: By material

7. Select **By material** on the **Color** drop-down menu.
8. The black lines of the crown molding will show in white. You can repeat the procedure with each of the materials and faces.
9. Save the file.

7.3.2 Face Settings

SketchUp contains a variety of face rendering styles allowing you to manipulate the amount of material and textures displayed on the screen.

1. In the **Style** window select **Default Styles** and choose **Engineering Style**.
2. Open **View / Face Style / Monochrome** (you can also select several face styles from the Style window).
3. Open the **Style** window and select the **Edit** tab.
4. Click on **Face Settings** button. Change colors for Front color and Back color. The Front color button sets the default color for all front sides of faces. Materials assigned to faces override this setting.
5. At this point probably you will have visible some faces with the front color and other faces will show the back color.

Note: When you export your model to other programs, such as 3D Studio, you will need to "reverse" all the faces to the front side to apply materials on that program.

13

(3)(4)   (5)

6. To reverse faces **select** them and **right-click / Reverse Faces**.

(Mac) After you choose a new face color in the **Colors** window close it or re-click the color box in the Style window.

7. Activate the **Shaded Using Textures** style from View / Face Style / Shaded with Textures or click on the icon.

8. It is probable that your model will continue to show some faces in flat color instead on the texture that you applied. When you reverse the faces you sent the textures to the back side.

9. **Orbit** around to see both sides of your faces. You can sample the textures on the back and reapply them on the front. If you do not intend to export your model, you can reverse the faces again with the same procedure explained on point 6.

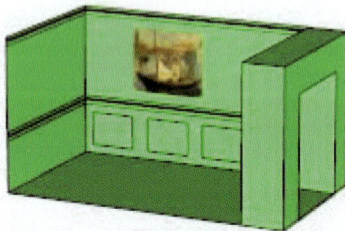

(6)

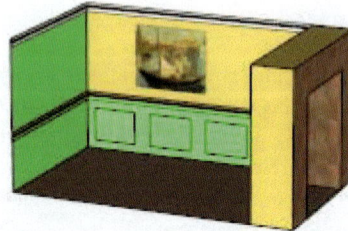

(8)

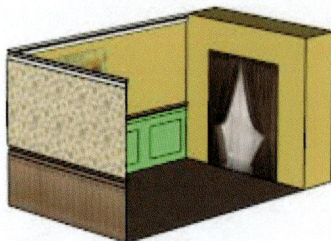

(9)

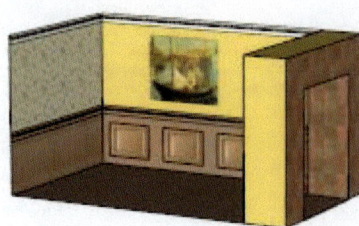

10. Use **Wireframe** mode to display the model as a collection of lines. Faces are not displayed in Wireframe mode. You cannot use face modification tools, such as the Push/Pull tool, on a wireframe rendered model

*Note: The **Transparency quality** option on Face Settings allows you to select the quality of transparency display between faster, medium, and nicer. Each option differs in its speed and quality of transparency sorting.*

7.3.3 Background settings

Styles also contain options for configuring the drawing area background, sky, and ground colors.
Use the **Background** button to select a background color for SketchUp's drawing area. Click on the box and choose a color.

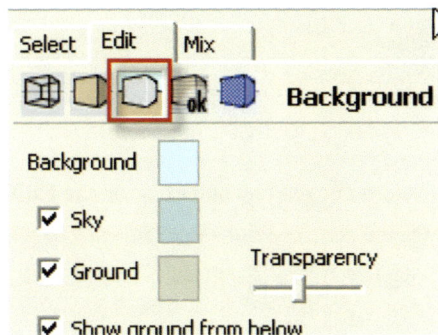

Use the **Sky** checkbox to have a sky color that is different from the background color. Use the Sky button to select a sky color.
Selecting the **Ground** checkbox selects a ground color that is different from the background color.

7.3.4 Watermark settings

Watermarks are images placed in the background or foreground of the drawing area and span the entire area just as sky and ground. Watermarks are great for creating backgrounds, such as simulating paper textures beneath a model. Watermarks can also be used to place logos and other graphics directly on the screen, or apply a landscape image to be viewed from a window.

1. Select **Window / Styles**. The Styles Browser is displayed.
2. Click on the **Edit** tab.
3. Click on the **Watermark** panel button. The Watermark panel is displayed.
4. Click on the **Add button**. The Choose Watermark dialog box is displayed.
5. Navigate to the resources folder and select **watercolor_tile_mask4.png**.
6. Click the **Open** button. The image will appear as a watermark on your model area. The Create Watermark dialog box is displayed.
7. Click the **Overlay** button to have the image appear in front of your model as an overlay.
8. Click on the **Next** button.
9. Move the **Blend slider** to the left to fade the watermark. (Move the Blend slider to the right to fade the model).
10. Click on the **Next** button.
11. Select **Tiled across the screen** and adjust the scale to select a desired grain.
12. Click on the **Finish** button.

(12)

13. To change the properties of the watermark select it and click on the **Edit Watermark Settings** button.

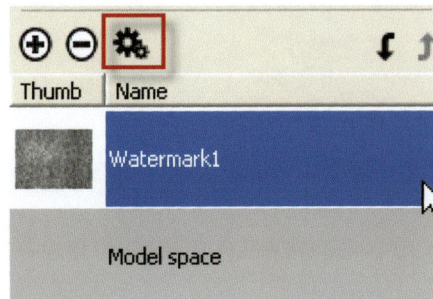

Note: If you want to save this style for further use, go to the In Model window, click on Update button, write a name and proceed to save it as a new collection.

To change settings of an existing style

14. Open the **Select** tab and open Assorted Styles collection.
15. Select **PSO vignette** thumbnail.
16. Open the **Edit** tab/**Watermark Settings**.
17. Select the gradient border and click on the down button to place it on second place.
18. Choose the **Grain overlay** watermark and select the **Edit Watermark Settings**.
19. Slide the scale slider to see other results.
20. Save your file as Tut_7.3.4

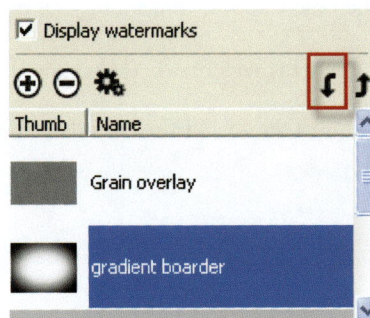

Chapter 8. How to manipulate your point of view

Objectives

When you have completed this chapter you will be able to:

- Walk around and make perspectives at any eye level.
- Use the following commands: Position Camera, Look Around, Walk, Perspective, Focal Length/Field of View

With the Position Camera tool you can position your view at a specific eye height so that you can check the line of sight of a model or walk through a model. Activate the Position Camera tool from either the Walkthrough toolbar (Microsoft Windows), Tool Palette (Mac OS X) or the Camera menu.

The camera is positioned using one of two methods. The first method places the camera at eye-level above a specific point (5' 6" above that point by default). The second method places the camera at a specific point, facing a specific direction.

8.1 Camera at eye level (   )

1. Open "ArtGallery" file or open your Components window, type "Art Gallery by agra" and download it into your model.

2. **Orbit** around to get a view similar to the one shown below.

3. Select the **Position Camera** tool. Notice that the Measurements toolbar indicates that the eye height above the ground plane is set to 5'-6". You can override this height at this time by typing in a desired value and then clicking Enter.

4. Click on a point in your model. SketchUp places the camera's point of view at an average eye-height over the point you click on. The following image shows a point in the middle of the room (check that you have **Camera / Perspective** option selected).

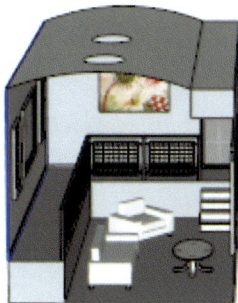

(2)

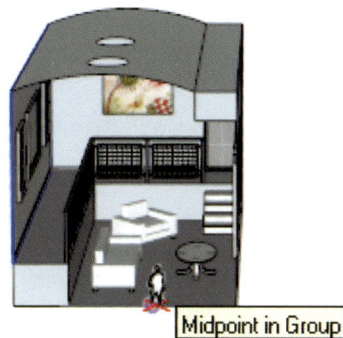

Midpoint in Group

(3)

(4)

8.2 Look Around ( )

1. The **Look Around** tool will be activated immediately. You will see a couple of eyes on your screen indicating this mode.
2. **Hold down** the left mouse button and move the view toward both sides, and up and down.
3. Click on the **Zoom** tool to change the **Focal Length/Field of View**.
4. Type 50. Enter.

(1)

(4)

8.3 Positioning the Camera Using Specific Target Points

This method allows you to position the camera at a specific point, facing a specific direction.

1. Select the **Iso** view and orbit around to have an aerial view from your model.

2. Select the **Position Camera** tool. The cursor changes to a small person with a red X. Notice that the Measurements toolbar indicates that the eye height above the ground plane is set to 5'-6". You can override this height at this time by typing in a desired value.

Tip: Use the Tape Measure tool and the Measurements toolbar to drag parallel construction lines off edges to provide accurate camera placements.

3. **Click and hold** mouse button on a point in your model.
4. **Drag** the cursor to the portion of the model that you want to look at. A dotted line is extended from the point selected in step 2 to the portion of the model you want to look at.
5. **Release** the mouse button. The camera is repositioned at a height of 0' at the point selected in step 2 since you did not locate any guide lines. The camera faces the item you dragged the cursor to in step 3. The following image shows a point in the middle of a room with a dotted line to the window on the left wall of the room. The camera will be positioned directly at the first point (with a height at zero).
6. **Type** 5'6" to readjust the eye level. Enter.

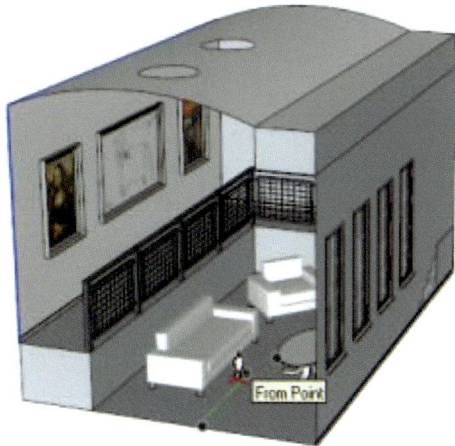

(2)(3)   (4)

8.4 Walk tool

1. Select the **Walk** tool.
2. Hold down the **left mouse** button while moving the cursor to the bottom of your screen to walk back.
3. **Move** the cursor up to the top part of your screen to walk forward.

Note: Use the Walk tool to maneuver through your SketchUp model as though you were walking through your model. Specifically, the Walk tool fixes the camera at a particular height and then allows you to maneuver the camera around your model. The Walk tool is available only in Perspective mode. Activate the Walk tool from the Walkthrough toolbar (Microsoft Windows), Tool Palette (Mac OS X) or the Camera menu.

Chapter 9. How to reach the inside of your model and create sections

Objectives

When you have completed this chapter you will be able to:

- Create sections.
- Use the following commands: Section tool, Section Plane, Section Cuts, Reverse section cuts, Align View, Create Group from Slice, Export Section Slice, Active Cut, Hidden Geometry.

9.1 Basics of Section tool

Use the **Section Plane** tool to create section cuts enabling you to view geometry within your model. This is a powerful tool for interior design and access to different views without having to hide or unhide objects.

1. **Open** "ArtGallery" and complete the missing wall. Unhide any group that you might hidden before.
2. Create a group and rename it as **"front wall"**. If you downloaded the model from the 3D Warehouse, the front wall is already drawn and hidden.
3. **Save** the file.
4. Accessing the interior space will be difficult unless you divide your geometry in different groups as you have done by now or you use the **Section** tool to avoid having so many groups, especially if you are handling a big project.

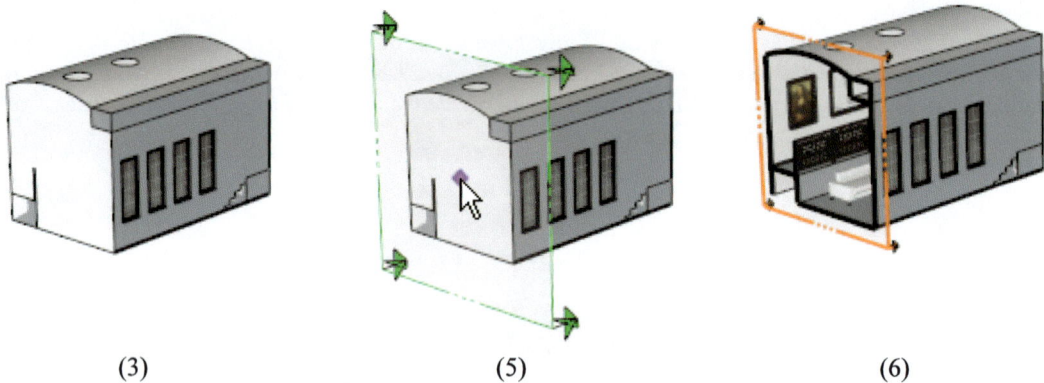

(3)   (5)   (6)

5. Activate the **Section Plane** ⬡ tool from the Guide Toolbar (Microsoft Windows), the Tool Palette (Mac OS X) or the Tools menu. The cursor changes to a pointer with a section plane (press the **Esc** key at any point during the operation to start over).
6. **Click** on a face to create a Section Plane entity and resulting section cut effect. The section plane will create a section slice in all entities in the current context and, therefore, the slice will expand to cover all entities in the context. The arrows point in the direction of the section view.

Note: You can change the appearance of the section plane by opening the Styles window/Edit/Modeling Settings/Active Section-Section cuts.

7. **Select** the selection plane. Move it inside with the **Move** ✳ tool (you can use any editing tool with a section plane: move, erase, copy, rotate and hide).
8. Turn off the Section plane by selecting **View** menu/uncheck **Section Planes**.

9. Active the **Sections** toolbar  by clicking on **View** menu/**Toolbars/Sections**. Turn on the Section Planes again.
10. Toggle off **Display Section Cuts**.

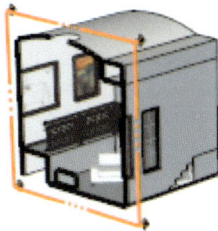  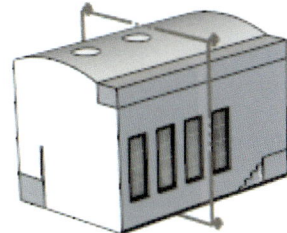

(7)   (8)   (10)

*Note: You can align the section plane with the face that you want and then hold down the **Shift** key to lock the orientation and click on any point to locate the section plane within your model.*

11. **Right-click** within the empty gray area or an outer edge of the section plane and select **Align View.** This aligns the section view with your screen. You can make any changes to the interior with the section cut active.

12. Select the **Iso** view 🏠 button.

13. **Right-click** on the outer edge of the section plane and choose **Reverse**. The formerly hidden part of the model appears.

14. **Orbit** around to see this section cut.

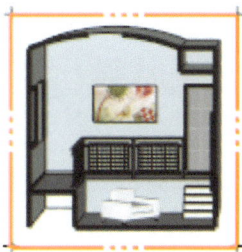 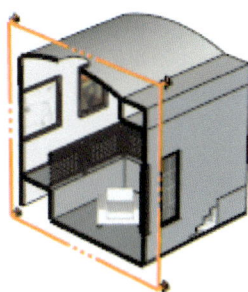 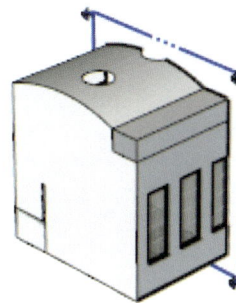 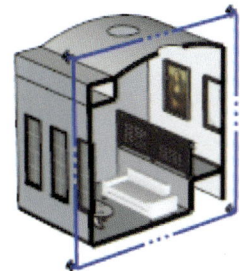

(11)   (12)   (13)   (14)

15. The section cut lines can be saved as a group. **Right-click** on the outer edge of the section plane.
16. Select **Create Group from Slice**. This creates a group of edges where the section plane hits the model. Hide the section plane to see the group. Hide all the groups on the **Outliner** except for the Group from Slice.

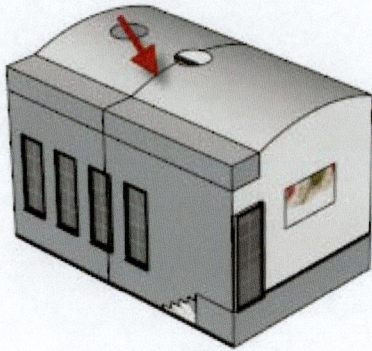

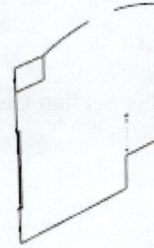

(16)   (16)

*Note: If you have the SketchUp Pro version you can export section slices. While a section plane is active, choose **File/Export/Section Slice**. You can export in dwg or dxf format. To specify conversion parameters, click on **Options**.*

17. Unhide all your geometry back.

18. Hide the Group from Slice. Toggle off **Display Section Cuts** .

19. Click on the **Section plane** tool again. Align the section plane with the outside wall that has 4 windows on it.

20. Hold down **Shift** key and move your section plane over the edge of the window on the back wall. Click.

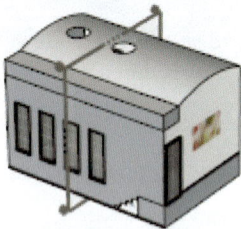

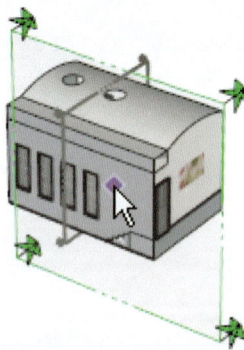

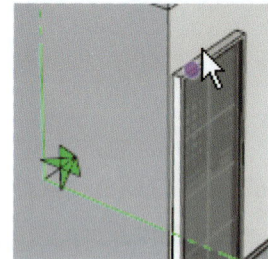

(18)   (19)   (20)

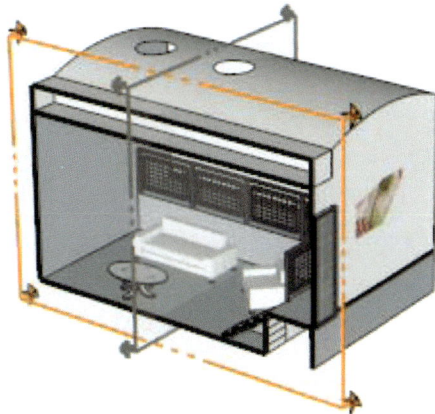

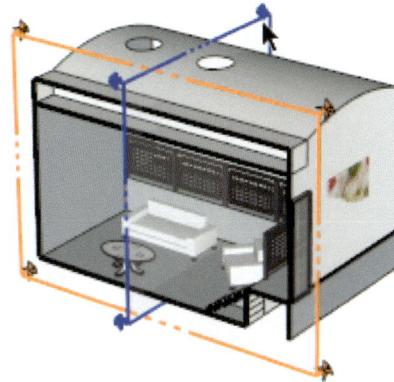

(20)   (21)

21. To be able to see the previous cut select the outer edge / **right-click** /**Active Cut**.

22. Click on the **Select** tool and double click on section cut along stairs. This will activate the section cut again.
23. **Right-click** on the transversal cut (it should be highlighted in blue) / **Hide**.
24. To recover the transversal cut click on **View/Hidden Geometry**. Select the section plane/right-click/Unhide.
25. Click again on **View**/uncheck **Hidden Geometry**.

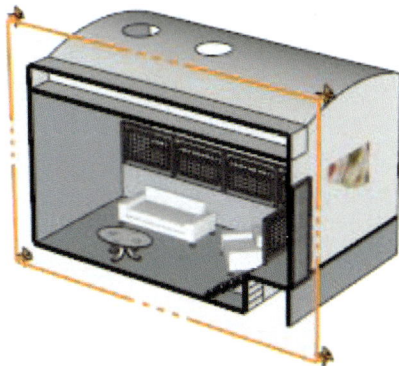

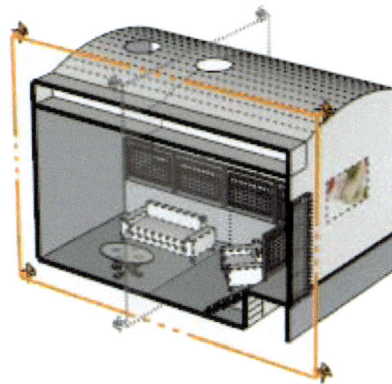

(23)   (24)

9.2 Simultaneous section cuts

SketchUp allows you to have only one section plane active per context. This means that you must place additional section planes within a group or component to have simultaneous multiple section planes active. Therefore, because they are in separate contexts, a section plane within a group or component can be active at the same time as a section plane outside of any group or component. A model with a group that also contains two other groups has four different contexts (one context outside of any group, one context inside the top level group, and one context each for the groups contained within the top-level group), and can have four active sections at once.

1. Toggle off **Display Section Cuts**.
2. Create a group with all your geometry except for the transversal cut.

3. Toggle on **Display Section Cuts**.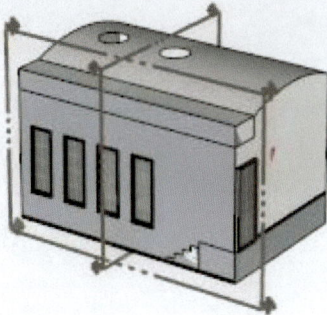

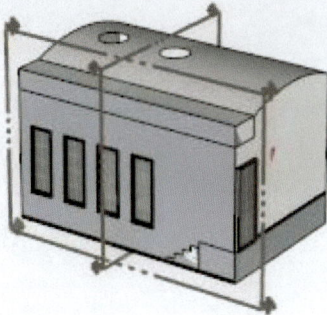

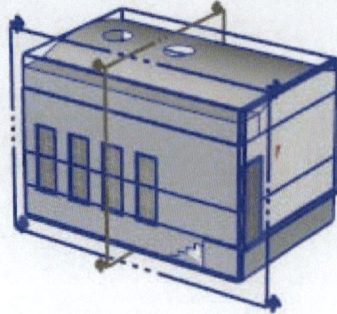

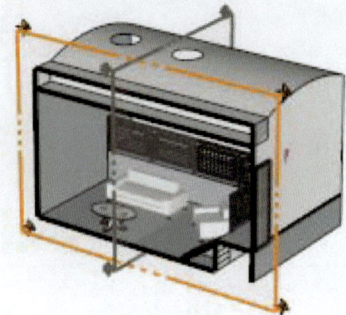

| (1) | (2) | (3) |

4. **Select** the transversal cut.
5. **Right-click / Active Cut**.

6. Toggle off **Display Section Planes**.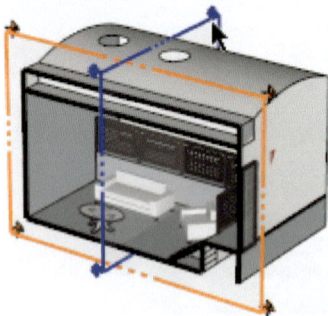
7. Save as Tut_9.2

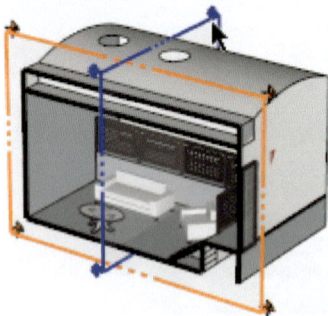

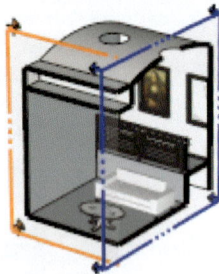

| (4) | (5) | (6) |

Chapter 10. How to save particular views of your model

10. Scenes

Objectives

When you have completed this chapter you will be able to:

- Save camera views so that you can retrieve them for later use.
- Use the following commands: Styles, Pre-defined styles, Edit styles, Style Settings.

You can use Scenes to save camera views, as well as several additional properties. You can store several properties with each scene:

- The view (camera position, zoom, and field of view).
- Shadow settings.
- Whether entities are hidden or displayed.
- Section planes.
- Drawing axes.
- Style Display Settings (display styles and edge effects).
- Layers.

Scenes store only properties, not geometry. There's only one instance of the geometry in a model, and all Scenes are simply views of that geometry. If you have a scene selected and draw some new geometry, you'll see the new geometry on every scene. The only things you can change from scene to scene are the properties that are stored.

However, there are some ways to use scenes with geometry in those cases when you need to show various options for furniture layout or color options that you will go through later.

When you add a scene, it inherits all the saved properties of the current scene. But if you're on an existing scene and make changes to any of the scene properties, you must update the scene in order to save the changes.

Components don't have Scenes. If someone creates a model with Scenes and shares it in the 3D Warehouse and you download that model directly into a SketchUp model, it comes in as a component. To be able to see and access Scenes, you must open the model in a new instance of SketchUp, so that it opens as a full model rather than as a component in a model.

10.1 Assigning styles to scenes and showing options through layers

Active style is automatically assigned to scenes you create in your SketchUp models.

1. Open "ArtGallery" and set to **Camera/Parallel Projection**.
2. Select the **Window > Styles** menu item. The Styles Manager is displayed.
3. Select the **Engineering style** from Default styles collection.
4. Open **View** menu/uncheck **Section Planes, Section Cuts** and **Axes**.
5. Select the **Top** view.
6. Open the **Outliner** and hide the ceiling group.
7. Select **Window / Scenes**. The Scenes Manager is displayed. In the lower part of the window are all the properties of your current view that you can save. By default all properties are checked.
8. Click the **Add Scene** ⊕ button. A scene is added to the list.

Note: If a warning message comes up before the scene is created you can choose "Do nothing to save changes" since you have not worked with scenes before this exercise. However, choosing this option will prompt you for the same question when you create a new scene.

9. The scene is automatically named "Scene 1". Enter a new name such as "Furniture Plan" in the Name field. Click outside the dialogue box.
10. A tab will be created under your top screen icons.

11. Click on the **Iso** view icon.
12. Return to the previous view by clicking on the "Furniture Plan" tab.

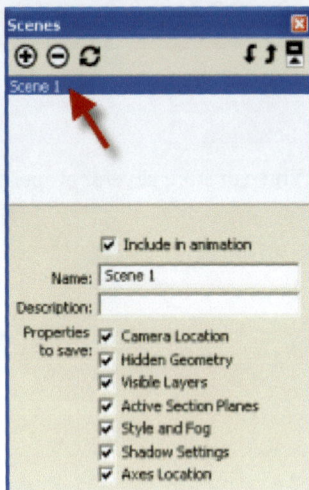

(8)

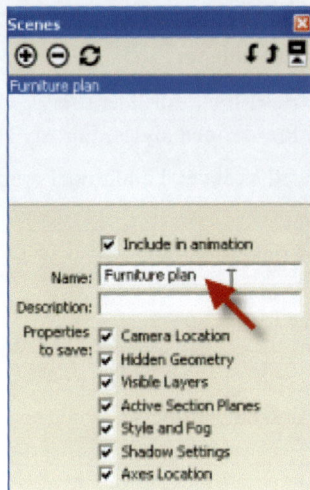

(9)

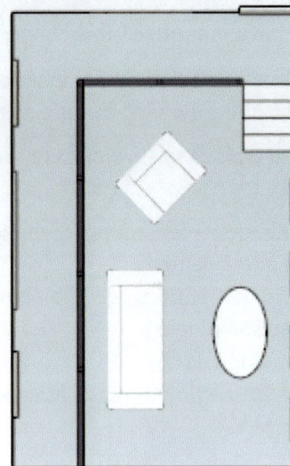

(12)

13. For the next scene open the **Layers** window and turn off the Furniture layer.
14. Open the **Scenes** window again.
15. Click on the **Add Scene** button / *"Do nothing to save changes".* Type a new name such as "Floor plan". Click outside the dialogue box.
16. Click on the Furniture plan tab. 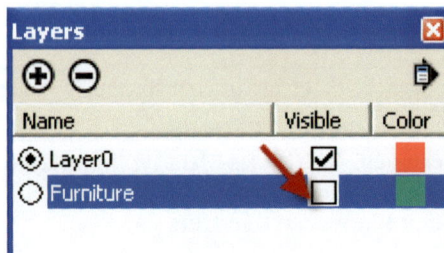 Furniture will show in this scene.
17. Click back on the Floor plan tab. Furniture will not show in this scene.

(13)

10.2 Updating a scene from the tab

1. Change to the **Iso** view.
2. Create another scene and name it "Iso".
3. Select "Save as a new style" option. Create.
4. Open the **Styles** window and select the Blueprint style from the Assorted Styles collection.

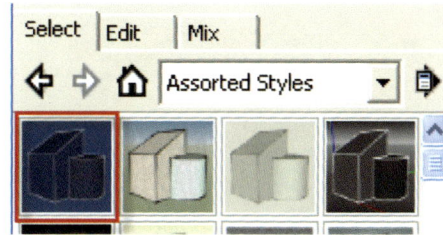

5. Click on **In Model** button and select the Blueprint icon.
6. Select the **Edit** tab / **Modeling Settings**. Uncheck **Section Planes** and **Section Cuts**.
7. Right-click on the **Iso** tab and select the **Update** option.
8. In the warning window choose "Update the selected style" / **Update scene** button.
9. Save your file as Tut_10.2.

(7)

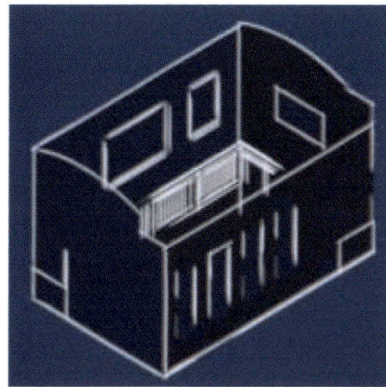

(8)

10.3 Changing a style assigned to a scene

1. Open Tut_10.2 and click on the **Furniture plan** tab on the left corner of your model screen.
2. Select **Window / Styles.** The Styles Manager is displayed.
3. Select the **In Model** styles from the drop-down list. The **In Model** styles are displayed.
4. Select the **Edit** tab / **Modeling Settings**.
5. Check the **Color by Layer** option. (uncheck Section Planes and Section Cuts)
6. Click the **Update Style with changes** button. The style is updated in all scenes that have the Engineering style.
7. Change the Style again by unchecking the **Color by Layer** option.

8. Click the **Update Style with changes** button. The style is updated in all scenes.
9. Save it as Tut_10.3.

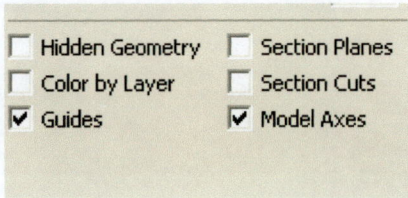

 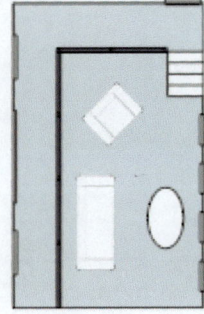

(5)   (6)   (7)

Note: You can use Scenes in multiple ways to achieve different results. Here are some ideas where you can use them

1. Create Section Animations:
    - To show a view of every level in a multistory building.
    - To show a construction process.
    - To get inside your model without having to hide different areas or groups, and show the relationship between several spaces.

Note: If you are planning to make section animations, remember to use a separate section plane for each scene. Sketchup will animate the transition between two different section planes. If you use the same section plane that has been moved from one place to another and add a scene, you will not get section animation.

2. Shadows study.
    - To show the sun's path during the year.

3. To show different camera locations, such as a transition from outside to an interior space.

4. To show or hide geometry, vegetation, objects or furniture.

5. To create a walkthrough inside your project.

6. To show options through layers.

4. To assign different styles.

Chapter 11. How to insert dimensions and texts and get information about your model

Objectives

When you have completed this chapter you will be able to:

- Get information about your model.
- Insert dimensions.
- Insert texts.
- Use the following commands: Model Info, Dimensions settings, Dimensions, Leader Text, Screen Text, Edit Text, 3D Text.

11.1 Model Info dialog box

The Model Info dialog box allows you to configure a number of different settings specific to your current SketchUp model.

1. Open Tut_10.3
2. Activate the **Model Info** dialog box from the **Window** menu.

The Model Info dialog box contains several panels, including the Dimensions panel for setting global dimensions and the Units panel for setting units to be used in your model.

11.2 Setting dimensions styles

1. Select Dimensions from the **Model Info** dialogue box.
2. Click on the **Fonts** button to select the font to be used for all Dimension entities in SketchUp. Select Arial Regular 10 / OK. The Text portion of the Dimensions panel allows you to select the font used by dimension entities in the drawing area.
3. Click on the **Font** color button to choose a font color for Dimension entities. Choose a red color from the color wheel.
   The Leader Lines portion of the Dimensions panel allows you to choose an end point style for your leader lines. Select **Slash** for the end point style for all of your end points from the **Endpoints** drop-down list. The available styles are None, Slash, Dot, Closed Arrow and Open Arrow.

4. Select the **Align to screen** option under Dimension. The **Align to screen** button allows Dimension entities to rotate as you orbit the model (always face the camera).
5. Close the **Model Info** dialogue box.

*Note: If you want to change the appearance of some or all dimensions in your model, use Select all dimensions button to select all dimension entities in the model. Make the desired changes and then **Update** selected dimensions.*

11.2.1 Inserting Dimensions

1. Click on the Floor plan tab.
2. Open the **Layers** window from the **Window** menu or your drop-down menu in your screen.
3. **Create** ⊕ a new layer called Dimensions. Set a color, make it current and leave it visible.

4. Select the **Dimension** tool.
5. Click on an end point and then click on the opposite side. Click outside for the dimension string placement.
6. Repeat the process on the long side.
7. Click on the **Iso** tab. As the model orbits around you will notice that the dimensions face the camera.

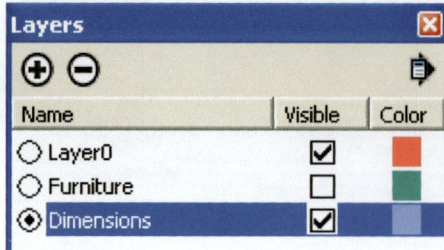

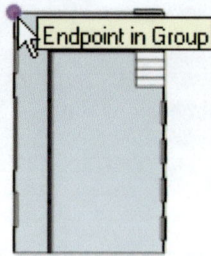

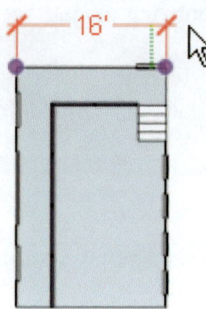

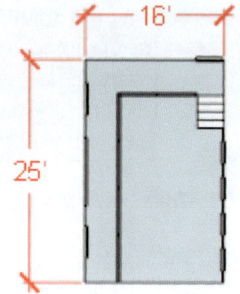

| (3) | (5) | (5) | (6) |

Note: Notice that the dimensions are referred to the top end point of the model instead to the bottom footprint. If you want to refer your dimensions to specific points, a better idea would be to activate the view that allows you to refer your points with accuracy.

8. Hide the front wall using the **Outliner** window.
9. Proceed to dimension the floor lines as shown below.
10. Return to the Floor plan view by clicking on the **Floor plan** tab.
11. Save as Tut_11.2.1.

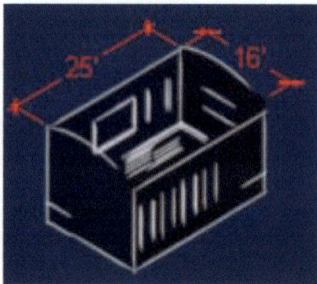

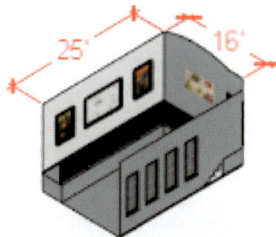

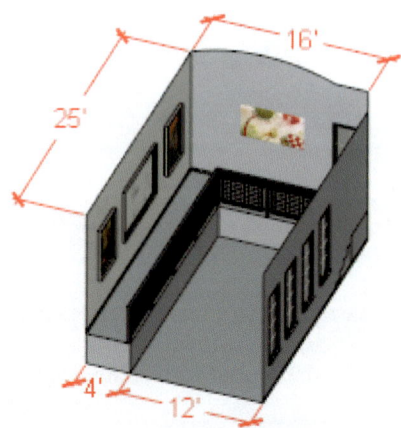

| (7) | (9) | (9) |

11.3 Text tool

Use the Text tool to insert text entities into your model. Activate the Text tool from either the Construction toolbar (Microsoft Windows), the tool palette (Mac OS X), or the Draw menu.

There are two types of text in SketchUp: Leader text and Screen text. Leader text contains characters and a leader line that points (refers) to an entity. Screen text contains characters and is not associated with an entity. It is fixed to the screen regardless of how you manipulate or orbit the model.

11.3.1 Creating and placing leader text

1. Open Tut_11.2.1.
2. Activate the **Model Info** dialog box from the **Window** menu. Select **Text** option.
3. Change the Font to Arial Regular 10 and pick a green color for the **Leader Text** section.
4. Close the **Text** dialogue box.
5. Open the **Layers** window. Create ⊕ a new layer called **Text**. Make it current, visible and assign a color.
6. Select the Furniture plan tab.
7. Activate the **Text** [ABC] tool. The cursor changes to an arrow with a text prompt.
8. Click on a sofa to indicate the ending point of the leader line (the location where the leader should point).

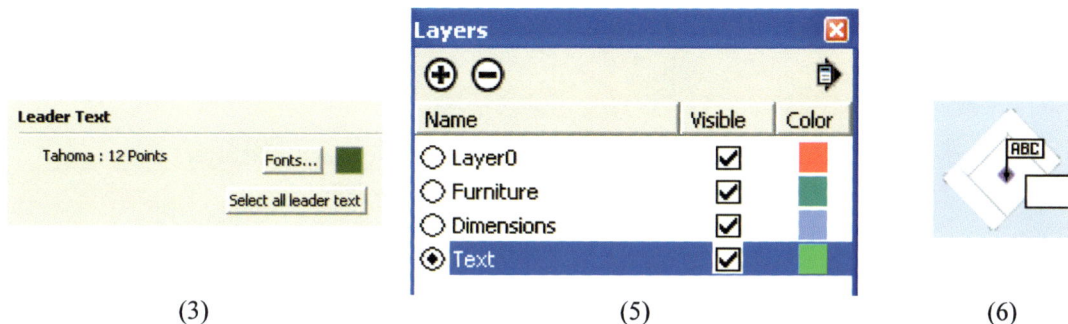

Leader Text
Tahoma : 12 Points   Fonts... ▣
Select all leader text

Layers ☒

⊕ ⊖   ▤

Name	Visible	Color
○ Layer0	☑	🟧
○ Furniture	☑	🟩
○ Dimensions	☑	🟦
◉ Text	☑	🟩

(3)   (5)   (6)

9. Move the cursor to position the text. The leader line will grow and shrink as you move the cursor around the screen.
10. **Click** to position the text. A text entry box appears with default text, such as the name of a component (if the ending point of the leader line is attached to a component), or the square footage of a square (if the ending point of the leader line is attached to the face of a square).
11. **Click** in the text box and type "Sofa Ref 3544".
12. Click outside of the text box, or press the Enter (Microsoft Windows) or Return (Mac OS X) key twice, to complete text entry.

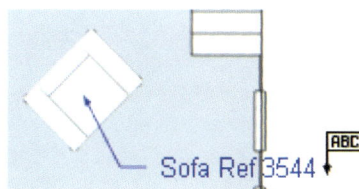

Sofa Ref 3544

Note: Press the ESC key at any point during the operation to start over.

11.3.2 Creating and placing screen text

1. Continue with the same file Tut_11.2.1.
2. Click on the **Furniture plan** scene tab.
3. Activate the **Model Info** dialog box from the **Window** menu. Select **Text** option.
4. Change the Font to Arial Regular 10 and pick a green color for the **Screen Text** section.

Screen Text

Arial : 10 Points   Fonts...   ▮

Select all screen text

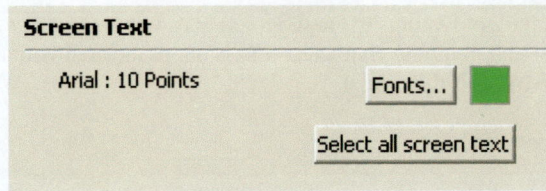

5. Select the **Text** [ABC] tool. The cursor changes to an arrow with a text prompt.
6. Move your mouse to the center of the space and click twice to open a text box.
7. **Write** "Lounge area".
8. **Click** outside of the text box, or press the Enter (Microsoft Windows) or Return (Mac OS X) key twice, to complete text entry. Screen text will stay fixed on the screen regardless of how you manipulate and orbit the model.

Lounge area

9. On the **Layers** window make the layer 0 current and turn off Dimensions and Text layers.
10. **Right-click** on the Furniture plan scene tab and choose the **Update** option.

⦿ Layer0   ☑   ▮
○ Furniture   ☑   ▮
○ Dimensions   ☐   ▮
○ Text   ☐   ▮

11. Click on the **Floor plan** tab.   Furniture plan Floor plan Iso
12. On the **Layers** window turn off Furniture and turn on Dimensions and Text layers.
13. **Right-click** on the **Floor plan** tab and choose the **Update** option. Using layers and scenes you can control visibility of parts of your project.

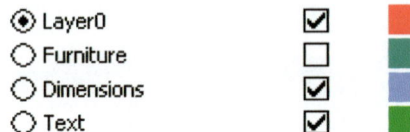

⦿ Layer0   ☑   ▮
○ Furniture   ☐   ▮
○ Dimensions   ☑   ▮
○ Text   ☑   ▮

11.3.3 Editing text

1. **Double-click** on the sofa text, with the **Text** tool or **Select** tool active, to edit the text. You can also right-click on a text entity and select the **Edit Text** menu item from the text entity's context menu.
2. Write "Sofa modern collection Ref 345".
3. Click outside of the text box.
4. Save as Tut_11.3.3.

11.3.4 3D Text

Use the 3D Text tool to create 3 dimensional texts. Activate the 3D Text tool from the Construction Toolbar (Microsoft Windows), the Tool Palette (Mac OS X) or the Tools menu.

1.   Open Tut_11.3.3.

2.   Select Iso [icon] view.

3.   Open the Layers window and check off Dimensions and Text layers.

4.   Create [icon] a new layer called 3D Text. Make it current.

Name	Visible	Color
○ Layer0	☑	
○ Furniture	☐	
○ Dimensions	☐	
○ Text	☐	
⊙ 3D Text	☑	

5.   Select the **3D Text** [icon] tool.

6.   Type "Art Gallery" in the text field.

7.   Check the **Extruded** option. Optionally, modify other settings.

8.   Click on the **Place** button. You are placed in a move operation with the 3D text and the move tool. If the text is too big, you can also scale your text after inserting it.

9.   Move the 3D text to the left wall.

*Note: The text is created as a component and will be aligned to any face. However, there is a small distance between the text and the face where it is lying. Because of this, you will not be able to intersect the letters with the model in case you need an engraved text. In case you need to vary distances of the extruded letters, edit the component and then use the **Pull/Push** tool.*

If you need to create an engraved text, do the following:

1.   Select the **3D Text** [icon] tool.

2.   Type your text in the text field.

3.   Uncheck Filled option. This alternative will situate your text on face, and no distance between the text and the face will be present. With this option you will be able to work with Intersect Selected or you can explode the text and push the letters inside a surface.

4.   Click on the **Place** button.

Chapter 12. How to incorporate shadows

Objectives

When you have completed this chapter you will be able to:

- Manage shadows in an indoor space.
- Do a shadow study.

Use the following commands: Location, Shadows Settings, Display Shadows, Use Sun for Shading, Light and Dark sliders

Shadows

The SketchUp Shadow tool gives you a general idea of how the sun and shadows affect your model during the course of a day and throughout the year. The calculations are based on the latitude and longitude. Because the lines of some actual time zones zigzag rather dramatically, the automatically calculated time zone for some locations may be off by an hour. In a few cases, the variance can be even longer. You can set the location and directional orientation by importing an image from Google Earth:

1. Install Google Earth to use this feature.
2. Open Sketchup. File / Geo-Location / Add Location. Type the address / Search. Click on Select Region button. Grab the piece of picture that you want to bring into your model.
3. The SketchUp model is now set to the same latitude and longitude as the location in Google Earth. The imported terrain image is aligned with the axes in SketchUp (the solid green axis points north and the solid red axis points east).

Note: You can access the same tool by clicking on the icon on the left bottom corner of your screen *. You need only to check "Use georeferencing" if you plan to export your model to Google Earth.*

You can also manually set the location, time zone, and solar orientation:

1. Open the "**Window**" menu.
2. Click "**Model Info**."
3. In the left pane, click "**Geo-Location**."
4. In the right pane select Set Manual Location. You can type a country, location, latitude and longitude.

Pro version feature: You can also manually control the solar orientation by entering the number of degrees it should vary from the default north direction in SketchUp (the direction the solid green axis points).

Open View menu / Toolbars / Solar North.

Select Toggle North Arrow icon. An orange axis will show your actual north orientation.

Click on North Set tool to change to a new solar orientation. Click on your screen and then point to your north. You can also choose Enter North Angle and type the degrees deviation from the green axis.

Free version plugin: Sketchup 8 (Free) does not offer to set the solar orientation. Since in Google SketchUp® the only source of light is the one coming from the sun you will need to set the light manually in many occasions. In Google SketchUp® 8 (Free) north is fixed in alignment with the internal Y-Axis. The green drawing Axis is aligned with north when the drawing axes are in their default position. So for those that work in the free version rotate the model to achieve the relationship to north you require. Then use the Axes tool to position the Drawing Axes to suit working on the model. Take into account that wherever the Drawing Axes are positioned, north always remains aligned with the internal Y-Axis. You can also install Jim's Model Location plugin. You can download it from http://sketchuptips.blogspot.com/2008/01/plugin-model-location.html. You need to install the two files in the Plugin folder.

12.1 Doing a shadow study

1. **Open** Tut_10.3.
2. Click on the **Iso** tab and change the style to Engineering Style.
3. Select **View/Section Planes**.
4. If you have the longitudinal section plane **select and double click** on it to open the group.
5. **Erase** the section plane.
6. Click outside the group to close it.
7. Create or select the transversal section plane and **move** it toward the stair landing (reverse the section cut if needed).

  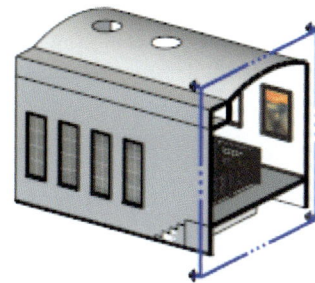

(4)   (5) (6)   (7)

8. Change to a **Top** view ⬚. Unhide the hidden ceiling using the outliner.
9. Check off **View/Section Planes** and **View/Section Cuts**.
10. Display the **Shadow Settings** window by clicking on **Window/Shadows**.
11. Set the **Time** slider to 10 AM and July 1st for **Date,** and **Time Zone** -5:00.
12. Click on the **Show/Hide Shadows** button. A shadow of the entire building will be projected on the ground.

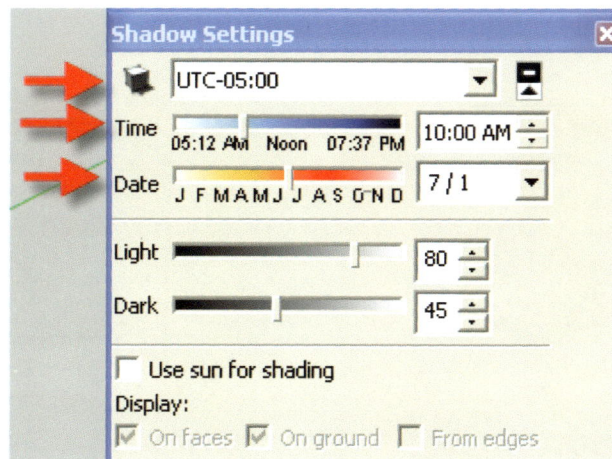

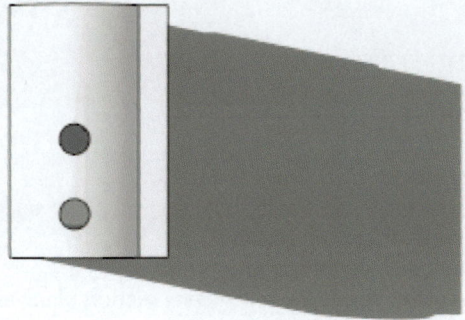

(12)   (13)

13. Slide the time toward the evening. You will notice that the shadows will be on the east side of the building.

To see the result of the shadows inside the room you will need to set an appropriate view.

14. Check off the **Show/Hide Shadows** button. Having the shadows on can slow down the performance of your computer. SketchUp recalculates the shadows anytime you make a change. Turn the shadows off while you are working in your model, and on when you need to see a shadows result.
15. Set **Camera/Perspective**.
16. Turn on **View / Section Cuts**.

17. Orbit around and select the **Position Camera** tool.
18. Click on the face of the hallway level.

19. Adjust the perspective with Walk and Look Around .

*Note: If at some point when you are using the Walk tool you cannot go back further, it means that you have active the collision detection. Disable it with the **Alt** key.*

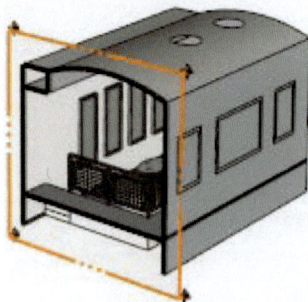

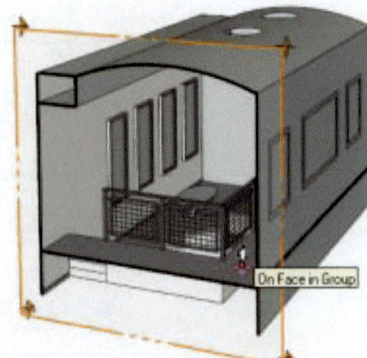

(16)   (17)

36

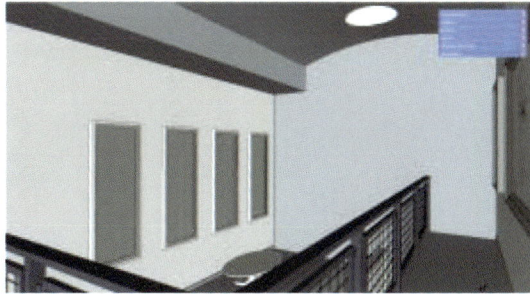

20. Open the **Shadow Settings** window. Check the "**Display Shadows**" box.
21. Set the time to 6.00 am on July 1st.
22. Open the **Scene** window and create a scene with the name 6 am.

23. Open the **Shadow Settings** window.
24. Set the time to 10.00 am.
25. Open the **Scene** window and create a scene with the name 10 am (save it as a new style).
26. Repeat the same steps and create a scene for 3 pm and another one for 6 pm.
27. Click on each scene tab to see the result along the day.

(21)   (24)

(26)   (26)

28. Save the file as Tut_12.1 and keep it open for the next exercise.

12.2 How to work with light and shadows in an interior space.

You can use the **Shadows Settings** dialog box to control the contrasts in your model. Manipulating the **Light** and **Dark sliders** can make a huge difference in an interior scene. The **Light slider** controls the lightness of surfaces that are not in shadow. Sliding it to the left will show everything in shade. The **Dark slider** controls the darkness of shadows cast on surfaces and on the ground.

The **Use Sun for Shading** check box does not control shadows but affects the appearance of your model. When it is selected you see more contrast in your model view.

The sun is the only source of lighting that SketchUp has, so any shadows or light you use in indoor scenes have to come from it. With a ceiling in your room everything is dark. You could take your ceiling away but your interior model will lack of an important feature. There are some techniques that you can use to solve this problem.

1. Decrease the darkness of the shadows by sliding the **Dark slider** to the right. This option will brighten your view considerably.

2. Adjust the settings in the **Shadow Settings** dialog box until the sun is shining through the windows. You might need to change the **Solar Orientation** as explained in the beginning of this chapter.
3. Create a ceiling that does not cast shadows. That will allow sunlight to shine directly onto your objects, casting their shadows. To make it seem like overhead lighting, set the time of day to noon on June 21st.

To create a ceiling that does not cast shadows:

4. **Select** the ceiling (you might need to double-click on the group to reach the ceiling instance).
5. Right-click / **Entity Info**.

6. Uncheck **Cast Shadows** box.
7. Move the **Dark Slider** over 50.
8. Repeat the steps with faces and objects that are casting undesirable shadows, such as ceiling lights, windows and walls.
9. Save as Tut_12.2.

Note: If you do not want to display any shadows, deselect the **Show/Hide Shadows** *button to turn off shadows. Select the* **Use Sun for Shading** *option and slide the* **Dark** *and* **Light** *sliders to add more contrast. Move the Time slider until things look good.*

Chapter 13. How to create an animation

Objectives

When you have completed this chapter you will be able to:

- Create an animation.
- Use the following commands: Play animation, Enable Scene Transitions, Export Animation.

13.1 Creating Animations

Animations are a series of scenes that are displayed in succession to give a hands-free tour of a model. You can use animation for a walkthrough of different areas or rooms of your projects. You can also show a construction process or different stages of your design.

1. Open Tut_12.1.

2. Select the **Back** view and be sure to have the perspective mode active.

3. Turn the shadows off in the **Shadows Settings** window.

4. Select **View**. Uncheck **Section Planes**. Use the Walkthrough tool to get an outside view as shown in the figure below.

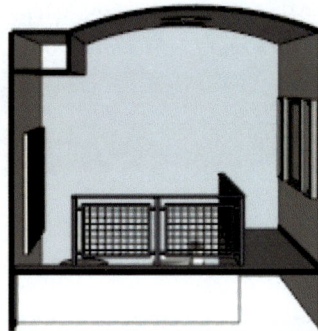

5. Click on **Window / Scenes**. The Scenes Manager displays.

6. Click the ⊕ button to add the scene. Type the name "Back Section" in the 'Name' field. Enter.

7. Save it as a new style if you are prompted to. A scene tab is added above the drawing window. The scene tab has the name of the scene you just assigned.

8. Check that the tab "Back Section" appears in the first place. If not, use the arrows on the Scene window to

   | Back Section | 6 am | 10 am | 3 pm | 6 pm |

   place it in the first row before 6 am tab.

9. **Right-click** on the Back Section tab above the Drawing Window. A context menu appears.

10. Select **Play Animation**. The animation cycles through each scene. You will see the transition from the outside to the inside, and the shadows will change along the day.

11. The **Animation** window allows you to pause at any moment or stop. On a Mac you can stop the animation by clicking on any scene tab.

You can also set the transition between the scenes:

12. Open **Window/Model Info/Animation**.
13. Change **Enable Scene transitions** to 3 seconds. Note that if this option is not checked the animation will jump from scene to scene. The Scene Delay is the amount of time each scene will be visible.
14. Save file as Tut_13.1 and leave it open for the next exercise.

13.2 Exporting Animations

Animation files can be used to present your model without the need for SketchUp. You can also import your files into another presentation or animation product to further enhance your animations. You can export an animation as an animation file or series of image files.

1. Select the **File / Export / Animation** menu item. The **Export Animation** dialog box is displayed.
2. Select the export type of your preference from the 'Export type' drop-down list according to your operating system.
3. Enter the name "Animation" for the exported file or series of files. The animation exporter will combine this name with a sequencing number for each image file that is created as part of a multiple image file animation. For example, if you export a 1 minute presentation called "myproject", at 10 frames per second, you will get 600 files, each named myproject0001.jpg, myproject0002.jpg, myproject0003.jpg all the way to myproject000600.jpg.
4. Click on the **Options** button. The **Animation Export Options** dialog box is displayed. The following image contains the Animation Export Options dialog box on Microsoft Windows:

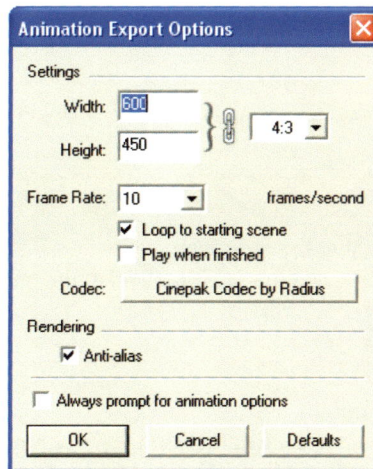

The following image contains the Animation Export Options dialog box on Mac OS X:

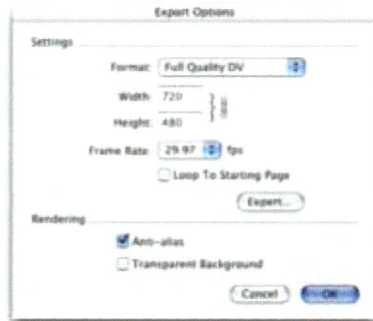

5. **Modify** Frame Rate to 15.
6. Click on the **Export** button to export the presentation as an animation. You can run your animation with any video program that you have installed in your computer.

SketchUp supports both single video animation file export (in the form of an Audio Video Interleave or AVI on Microsoft Windows and QuickTime on Mac OS X) and multiple image file export.

Practice Chapter 7 to 13

To consider:

Some required steps to complete all the practices might be omitted since the step- by -step explanation has been given in the tutorials. If you are unable to complete an exercise, refer to the according chapter.

Tools used: Section Plane, Styles, Views, Shadow Settings, Camera, Perspective, Position Camera, Walk, Solar orientation, Look Around, Animation, Export animation

Send an email to sketchup-interior-design@nextcad.net requesting this video. To get the file for next exercise open Sketchup. Open File menu / 3D Warehouse / Get Models. Type "gabled house by agra". Select Download Model.

1. Create a floor plan using section planes

Open the Gabled House file from the resources folder and activate the Iso view. Orbit around to have a view from the front porch.

1. Select the **Section Plane** tool.
2. Locate it on the porch floor to align it to the red-green plane.
3. Click and hold down the **Shift** key. Locate the section plane in the middle of a window. **Click**.
4. A section of the entire house will reveal the interior.

5. Select the **Top** view.
6. Open **View / Uncheck Section Planes**.
7. Open the **Styles** dialogue box and select the **Engineering style** on the Select tab of the Default Styles.
8. Open the **Edit / Modeling** tab and change the **Section cut width** to 1.

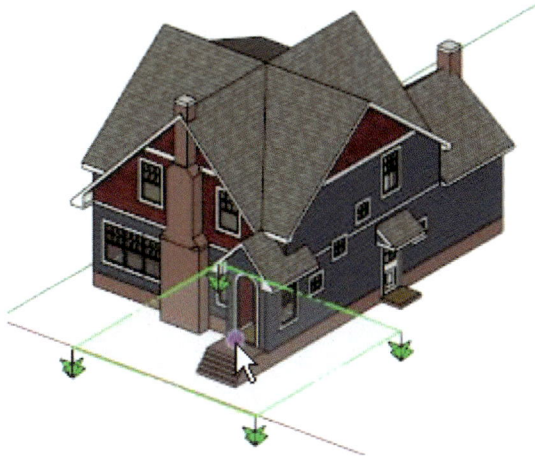

(2)

(3)

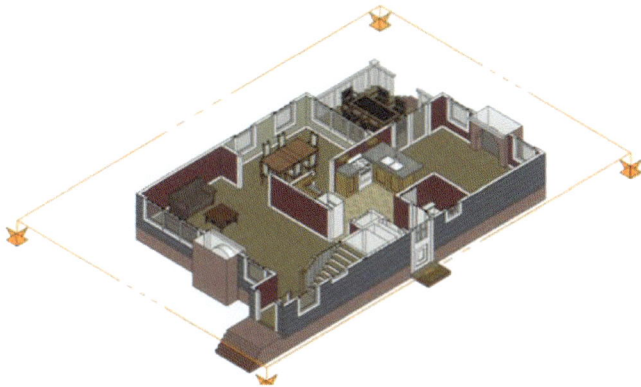

(4)

(8)

9. Open the **Shadows Settings** window.
10. Click on **Show/Hide Shadows** button, Time to 1 pm, Date to 6/21, Light to 80 and dark to 45.

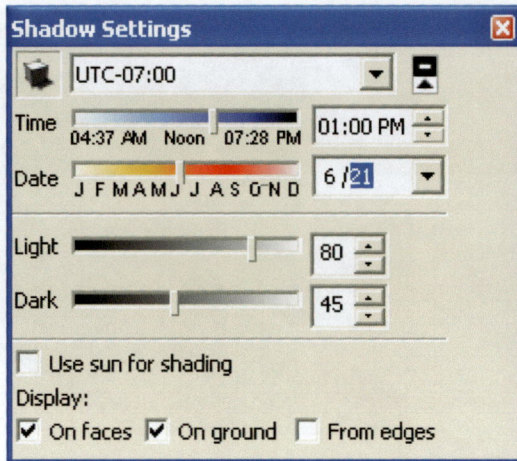

(10)

(11)

11. Open the **Scenes** window. Add a scene named Floor plan. Create a new style.
12. Save as Pr_7.1 Keep it open for the next exercise.

2. Create a cross section using section planes

1. Repeat the procedure to create a vertical cross section as shown below. Activate the Section Plane tool; place it on the right elevation. Change to the right view.
2. Set on **Camera / Parallel projection**.
3. Create a scene called Cross Section. Save it as a New Style.
4. Click on **View / Uncheck Section Planes**.
5. Save as Pr_7.2. Keep it open for the next exercise.

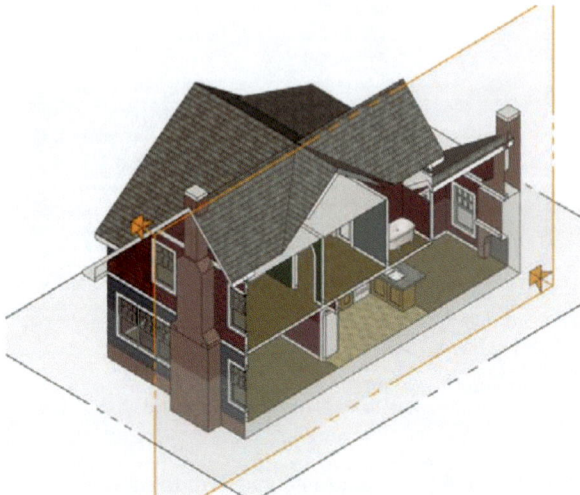

(1)

(2)

3. Create an interior perspective

1. Choose **Camera / Perspective** on the Cross Section tab.

2. Select the Position Camera tool and click on the floor edge of the living room area.

44

3. Select the **Walk** 👣 tool. Walk back until the collision detection does not allow you to go farther.
4. Create a new scene named "Perspective".
5. Save as Pr_7.3. Keep it open for the next exercise.

Midpoint in Component

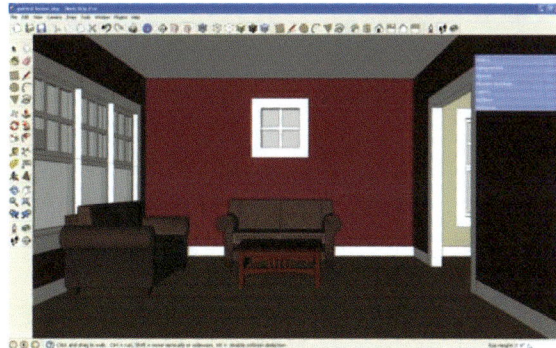

(1)(2)   (3)

4. Allow shadows and sun light to come in through the window (Pro version)

1. Set your model on the **Top** view.
2. Select **View / Toolbars / Solar North**.

3. Select the Set North Tool 🌞 .
4. Point the North arrow toward the NW. By default the North points the green direction if you have not changed your model axes; otherwise it will point to the upper part of your screen.
5. Click on the Perspective tab to return to that view.
6. Open the **Shadow Settings** window.
7. Click on the **Show/Hide Shadows** button.
8. Change the setting to UTC-07.00, 1 pm on January, 1st. Modify the sliders until it looks good.
9. Save.

Note: If you have Sketchup 8 (Free) and have installed Jim's Model Location plugin as explained in page 35, you can set the angle of the solar orientation and follow the exercised explained above.

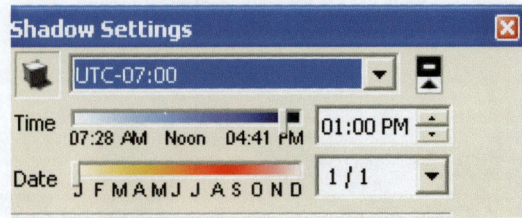

(1)(2)(3)(4)   (9)

Note: Any changes that you make on a scene that you want to keep for further use must be updated. To update a scene enter the ***Scenes*** *window and click on the* 🔄 *button to update it.*

5. Create an animation

1. Open Pr_7.3
2. Uncheck **Show/Hide Shadows** button.
3. Being in the Perspective tab, select the **Position Camera** 🧍 tool.
4. Click near the opening next to the dining room. The **Look Around** 👁 tool will be activated.
5. Move your mouse to the right to turn around and look toward the dining room.
6. Select the **Walk** 👣 tool to move back.
7. Create a new scene. Name it Dining room.
8. Disable **Section Planes** and **Section Cuts** from the View menu.
9. Repeat the last steps to create 3 more views.

(5)

(8)

(8)

(8)

10. Click on the Floor Plan tab. **Right click / Scene Manager**. Uncheck **Include in animation** box.
11. Repeat the same steps for the cross section tab.
12. Save as Pr_7.4
13. Click on the Perspective tab. **Right-click / Play Animation**. Correct any problems in each of your scenes and update the tab if you make any changes.
14. Open **File / Export / Animation**. Write a name and click on the Options button for any changes on export options.
15. Click on the **Export** button.

Chapter 14. How to print your work and share it

Objectives

When you have completed this chapter you will be able to

- Print scenes and different model views.
- Print in a determined scale.

Use the following commands:

SketchUp allows you to print your designs using any printing device. You can also print to scale and span a print across multiple sheets, allowing you to output a large drawing from a standard printer.

14.1 Basic steps to print on Microsoft Windows

1. Open the Gabled House file and select the Iso scene.

2. Use **Zoom Extents** to center your drawing in your window. Using this command you will be able to center your drawing within your paper. If at some point you find that your drawing is coming out on several pages instead of being centered in the selected paper size, go back to your screen and use **Zoom Extents**.
3. Select the paper size for your printer using **File / Print Setup**. Choose your printer, paper size and orientation.
4. Click on **File / Print Preview**.
5. In the **Tabbed Scene Print Range** choose the scenes that you are going to print. If you have only one scene in this part of the dialogue box, it will not be enabled.
6. In the **Print Size** section choose **Fit to page.** The **Fit to page** option is used to size the model to fit on a single sheet of paper and will tell SketchUp to make your printed page look like your Modeling Window. This option must be disabled to specify a different size or scale.
7. Check the **Model Extents** option to instruct SketchUp to zoom in to make your model fit the printed page.

*Note: As long as you do not have the **Fit to page** option selected you can manually enter a page size using **Page size**. If you type in a width or a height, the other dimension will be calculated. Use this option to make a larger picture by tiling together many smaller pages.*

8. Click on the OK button. You will see an image of what your print will look like.
9. If you are satisfied with the result, click on the **Print** button. You can also close the preview window and then print your model using **File / Print**.

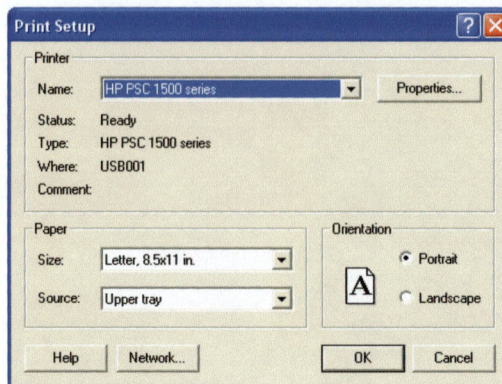

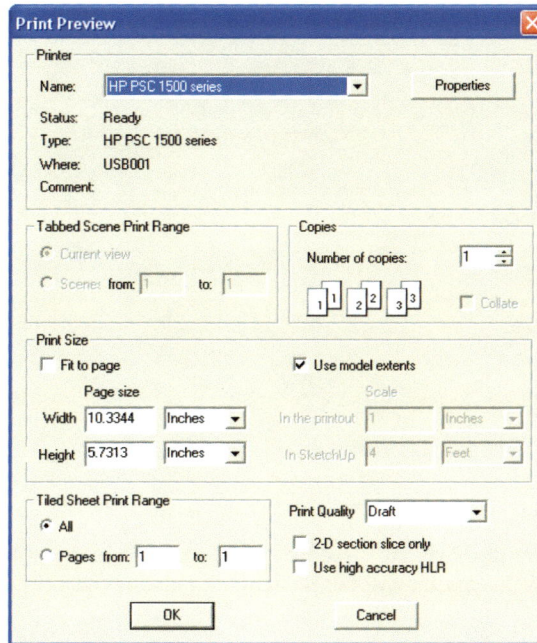

Fit to page

Fit to page + Use model extents

The Print Preview and Print dialog boxes contain the same series of options. The only difference is that the Print Preview dialog box outputs your model to the screen instead of to a printer. Items configured in one of these dialog boxes automatically appear in the other dialog box.

14.2 Basic steps to print on Mac OS X

1. Open Tut_10.2 and select the Iso scene.

2. Use **Zoom Extents** to center your drawing in your window. Using this command you will be able to center your drawing within your paper. If at some point you find that your drawing is coming out in several pages instead of being centered in the selected paper size, go back to your screen and use **Zoom Extents**.

3. Use **File / Page Setup** to select printer, paper size and orientation for your printer.
4. Click on the **OK** button.

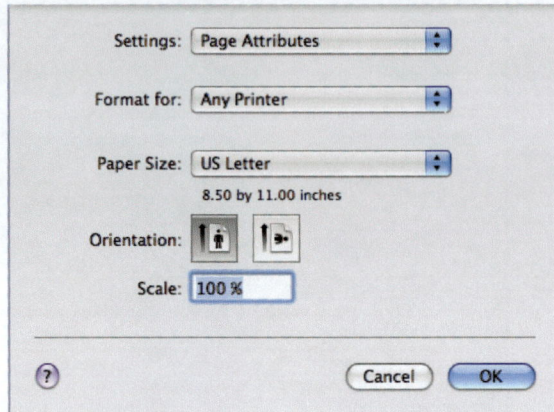

5. Choose **File / Document Setup**. Make sure that the **Fit View to Page** check box is selected.
6. Click the **OK** button. Using this option will tell SketchUp to make your printed page look like your Modeling Window.

*Note: As long as you do not have the **Fit View to Page** option selected you can manually enter a page size using **Print size**. If you type in a width or a height, the other dimension will be calculated. Use this option to make a larger picture by tiling together lots of smaller pages. The Pages Required section is a readout of the number of pages you need to print. With the **Fit View to Page** box selected this should read:*

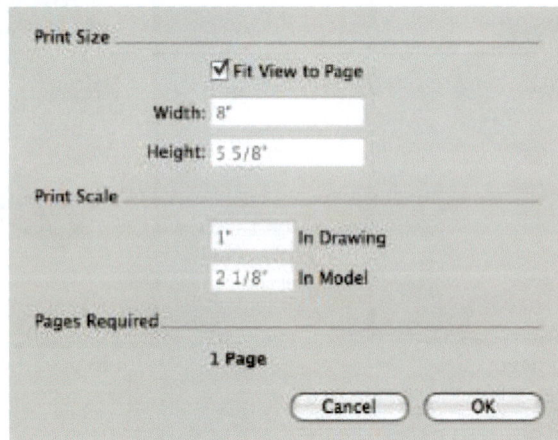

7. Use **File / Print**. Select 1 copy. If the Pages readout indicated that you need more than one page, you can choose to print some or all of them. In the Print dialog box click the **Preview** button. If you are satisfied with the result, click on the **Print** button.

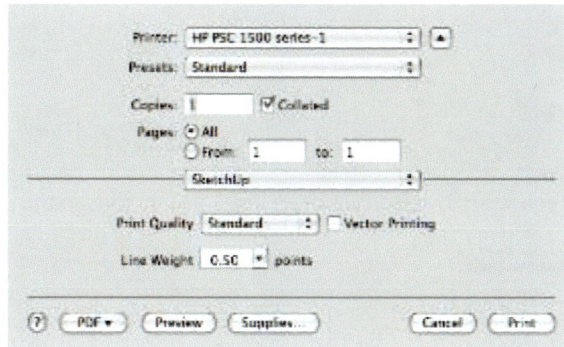

14.3 Printing to scale on Windows

Before printing to scale you have to set things up properly. Since perspectives views can not be printed to scale, switch to **Parallel Projection** on **Camera / Parallel Projection**. Choose any standard view, such as **Top** view.

1. **Open** Tut_11.2.1 and select the Furniture plan scene tab. Open the **Layers** dialog box and make Dimension visible. In this scene you should have a **Top** view in parallel projection.
2. Use **Zoom Extents** to center your drawing in your window. Using this command will enable you to center your drawing within your paper. If at some point you find that your drawing is coming out in several pages instead of being centered on the selected paper size, go back to your screen and use **Zoom Extents** and try a different paper **Orientation**.
3. Choose **File / Print Setup**. Select your printer, paper size and orientation. Click on the **OK** button.
4. Choose **File / Print Preview**.
5. Deselect the **Fit to page**. Although many savvy SketchUp users suggest deselecting **Use model extents** I have found that it is better to print on one sheet (if the scale is correct) by leaving it selected. Try both options for the Print preview step to see which one works better on your printer. The **Use model extents** option is used to print only the model as viewed using the **Zoom Extents** tool. This option might discard any surrounding empty background.

The Scale fields are used to scale your model for printing. The first measurement, labeled in the Printout, is the measurement of the exported geometry. The second measurement, labeled In SketchUp, is the actual measurement of the object in real scale. Enter the scale at which you would like to print. If you want to print at ¼" = 1' you have to enter **1 Inches In the Print out** box and **4 Feet** into In SketchUp box. Do not pay attention to the numbers that appear on the **Page size** option when you are printing to scale.

Here are some common scales configurations:

Architectural
½" = 1'. Enter 1 Inches; 2 Feet
¼" = 1'. Enter 1 Inches; 4 Feet
3/16" = 1'. Enter 3 Inches; 16 Feet
1/8" = 1'. Enter 1 Inch; 8 Feet

Engineering
1" = 20'. Enter 1 Inches; 20 Feet
1" = 50'. Enter 1 Inches; 50 Feet
1" = 100'. Enter 1 Inches; 100 Feet

Metric
1:20.= Enter 1 Meters; 20 Meters
1:50 = Enter 1 Meters; 50 Meters
1:100 = Enter 1 Meters; 100 Meters

6. Take note of how many pages your drawing needs by checking this information in the **Tiled Sheet Print Range** area on the dialog box. If you want to select a different size paper, change the settings in **File / Print Setup**.
7. Click the **OK** button and if you are satisfied click the **Print** button. You can also close the preview window and then print your model using **File / Print**.

14.4 *Printing to scale on Mac*

Before printing to scale you have to set things up properly. As perspectives views can not be printed to scale switch to **Parallel Projection** on **Camera / Parallel Projection**. Choose any standard view, such as **Top** view.

1. **Open** Tut_10.2 and select the Furniture plan scene tab. Open the **Layers** dialog box and make Dimension visible. In this scene you should have a **Top** view in parallel projection.

2. Use **Zoom Extents** to center your drawing in your window. Using this command will enable you to center your drawing within your paper. If at some point you see that your drawing is coming out in several pages instead of being centered in the selected paper size, go back to your screen and use **Zoom Extents** and try a different paper **Orientation**.
3. Choose **File / Page Setup**. Select your printer, paper size and orientation. Click on the **OK** button.
4. Choose **File / Document Setup**
5. Deselect the **Fit View to Page**.

The Scale fields are used to scale your model for printing. The first measurement, labeled **In Drawing**, is the measurement of the exported geometry. The second measurement, labeled **In Model**, is the actual measurement of the object in real scale. Enter the scale at which you would like to print. If you want to print at ¼" = 1' you have to enter **1 Inches In the Print out** box and **4 Feet** into In SketchUp box. Do not pay attention to the numbers that appear on the **Page size** option when you are printing to scale.

Look for the most common scale configurations in the previous item.

6. Take note of how many pages your drawing needs by checking this information in the **Pages Required** area on the dialogue box. If you want to select a different size of paper change the settings in **File / Page Setup**.
7. Click the **OK** button.
8. Open **File / Print**. Click on the **Preview** button and if you are satisfied click the **Print** button.

14.5 *Tiled sheet print range*

If the current scale is larger than the paper size of your printer or plotter, the entire model can be printed by printing on several pieces of paper. These pieces of paper can then be taped together to create the final scaled model. For example, tiling lets you print proofs of a large model, such as a B size (11" x 17"), on a printer that uses a smaller paper size, such as an A size (8.5" x 11"). Tiling also lets you print banners that are made up of multiple pages.

Tiling is available when you use the Scale fields to scale a model to be larger than the current paper size available in your printer.
You can also print selected page tiles within the set by entering a page number range in the Pages from fields. Page tiles are numbered top to bottom beginning at the top left of the drawing page.
You can display a preview of tile Pages using Print Preview in the File menu.
Printing large tiled output can be taxing on your computer's resources.

14.6 2D section slice only

The **2D section slice only** option in the **File / Print Preview** dialog box is used to output only the section slice outlines in your model (if present).

This is a **Pro** only feature.

To export a section slice:
1. Double-click on the Section Plane entity whose section slice you want to export.
2. Select File / Export / Section Slice. The Export 2D Section Slice dialog box is displayed   (Microsoft Windows).
3. Enter a file name for the exported file in the "File name" (Microsoft Windows) or "Save As" (Mac OS X) field.
4. Select the export type from the 'Export type' (Microsoft Windows) or 'Format' (Mac OS X) drop-down list.
5. (optional) Click on the Options button. The Section Slice Export Options dialog box is displayed.
6. (optional) Adjust the options in the Section Slice Export Options dialog box.
7. (optional) Click the OK button.
8. Click the Export button.

14.7 Use High Accuracy HLR

The Use High Accuracy HLR option in the File / Print Preview dialog box is used to send the model information to the printer as vector information. Vector lines look much smoother and cleaner when printed, except for shadows and rounded surfaces. Do not use this option if you are printing with a sketchy edge style.

14.8 Exporting files to other programs

To apply most of the following concepts you will need to have the Pro version of SketchUp. You will be able to export your files in 2D and 3D to different software. However, in this book you will find only explanation about the most common file types.

If you use the **Free Version** you can export 3D models to other programs in several 2D and 3D formats like JPEG image (.jpg), Portable Network Graphics (.png), Tagged Image File (.tif), Windows Bitmap (.bmp). You can also export your files to COLLADA (.dae) format for use in a variety of different 3D programs or place models in Google Earth. You can also export animations and walkthroughs as MOV with the Mac version of SketchUp, or export AVI files from the Windows version of SketchUp.
In addition to everything you can do with Google SketchUp®, using Google SketchUp® Pro you can export in additional 2D formats like Portable Document Format (.pdf), Encapsulated PostScript Format (.eps), Epix (.epx), Autocad® (.dwg, .dxf). The 3D formats are 3DS (.3ds), Autocad® DWG (.dwg), Autocad® DXF (.dxf), FBX (.fbx), OBJ (.obj), XSI (.xsi), VRML (.vrml),

14.8.1 Exporting animations

Animation files can be used to present your model without the need of SketchUp. You can also import your files into another presentation or animation product to further enhance your animations. You can export an animation as an animation file or series of image files.

To export animations refer to item **13.2 Exporting Animations.**

14.9 Exporting a PDF file

14.9.1 Exporting a PDF file (Microsoft Windows)

This is a Pro only feature. The PDF and EPS export is used to export vector SketchUp files for use in other vector-based editing programs, such as Adobe Illustrator. Some graphic features of SketchUp, including textures, shadows, smooth shading, backgrounds, and transparency, cannot be exported to PDF and EPS.

1. Select the **File / Export / 2D Graphic / Select PDF** for Export type.
2. Enter a file name for the exported file in the 'File name' field.
3. Click the **Options** button.

Full Scale (1:1) option is used to set your output to a 1:1 (real world) scale. Width/Height: are used to enter a custom page size for your file. Hidden-Line Output/In SketchUp fields work the same as the printing on scale.

The **Profile Lines** section of the PDF/EPS Hidden Options dialog box contains options for exporting profile lines. Show profiles exports any lines that are displayed in profile as thicker lines in the 2D vector file. All lines are output normally, without profile thickness, when this option is disabled, regardless of the screen display. Match screen display (Auto Width). The Match screen display (auto width) automatically sets the width of profile lines by matching the output to the proportions you see in the SketchUp drawing area. This option is available only when **Show profiles** is checked. The Width fields are used to specify an exact width for the profile lines. This option is available only when **'Show Profiles'** is checked and '**Match screen display** (auto width) is unchecked.

The **Section Lines** section contains options for exporting section lines. The Specify section line width option is used to adjust settings for Section Slice lines that are output. Match screen display (Auto Width). The Match screen display (auto width) automatically sets the width of section lines by matching the output to the proportions you see in the SketchUp drawing area. This option is available only when 'Specify section line width' is checked. The Width fields are used to specify an exact width for the section lines. This option is available only when 'Specify section line width' is checked and 'Match screen display (auto width)' is unchecked.

The **Extension Lines** section of the PDF/EPS Hidden Options dialog box contains options for exporting extension lines. The Extend edges option is used to toggle the export of line extensions. Match Screen Display (Auto Width) The Match screen display (auto width) automatically sets the width of extension lines by matching the output to the proportions you see in the SketchUp drawing area. This option is available only when "Extend edges' is checked. The Width fields are used to specify an exact width for the extension lines. This option is available only when 'Extend edges' is checked and 'Match screen display (auto width)' is unchecked.

The **Always prompt for hidden line** options is used to automatically display the Hidden Line Options dialog box when you export a 2D PDF or EPS file.

Map Windows fonts to PDF base fonts.
This option is used to select PDF fonts that correspond to the Windows fonts used in the model.

Defaults: This button is used to return the items in the Hidden Line Options dialog box to the default settings.

4. Accept all default options
5. Click the Export button.

14.9.2 Exporting a PDF file (Mac OS X)

1. Select the File / Export menu item. The export dialog box is displayed.
2. Enter a file name for the exported file in the 'Save As' field.
3. Select PDF from the Format drop-down list.
4. (Optional) Click the Options button. The PDF Export Options dialog box is displayed. Refer to the PDF Export Options dialog box (Mac OS X) for further information.
5. Click the Save button. The images are saved and then displayed in your current PDF viewer (by default).

14.10 Exporting Image files (Microsoft Windows)

1. **Select File / Export /** select any image file extensions from the Export type drop-down menu.
2. Enter a file name for the exported file in the 'File name' field.
3. (Optional) Click on the **Options** button to select a different image size.
4. Click the **Export** button.

14.11 Exporting 2D DWG or DXF Files

This is a **Pro** only feature.

1. **Select File / Export / 2D Graphic**. The Export 2D Graphic dialog box is displayed (Microsoft Windows).
2. Enter a file name for the exported file in the 'File' name (Microsoft Windows) or 'Save As' (Mac OS X) field.

Note: If you want to export the 3D geometry you will need to select File / Export / 3D Model.

3. Select the DWG or DXF export type from the 'Export type' (Microsoft Windows) or 'Format' (Mac OS X) drop-down list.
4. (optional) Click on the Options button. The DWG/DXF Hidden Line Options dialog box is displayed.
5. (optional) Adjust the options in the DWG/DXF Hidden Line Options (Microsoft Windows) or Export Options (Mac OS X) dialog box.
6. (optional) Click the OK button.
7. Click the Export button.

14.12 Importing files

You can import several types of 2D and 3D files by **File / Import**.
2D images: JPEG image (.jpg), Portable Network Graphics (.png), Tagged Image File (.tif), Targa File (*.tga), Windows Bitmap (.bmp).

3D models and information: SketchUp (.skp), Google Earth terrain, 3DS (.3ds).

Note: If you want a 3DS import to include textures, before the import you must save the texture files in the same folder as the 3ds file itself. ACAD files (.dwg, .dxf) are a Pro only feature. DEM (.dem, .ddf).

14.12.1 Importing an Autocad®® file

Before importing an Autocad®® file it is important to prepare it in an appropriate way so that you can use SketchUp. Delete texts, hatches and dimensions. SketchUp automatically discards any of these entities. Place all items in a single layer other than 0 unless for a specific reason you want to leave all the layers separated. Remember that layers in SketchUp have a different purpose from Autocad®®. Explode your blocks so you do not keep their layers. Purge all the elements in Autocad® and save the file. Be aware of the units you are using in Autocad®® and your Sketchup file. Once in SketchUp open a new file.

1. Select **File / Import / browse** for your resources folder.
2. Select **Autocad® files** in the drop-down menu.
3. Browse for **floor plan.dwg** inside the resources folder.
4. Click on the **Options** button and uncheck **Preserve drawing origin**. Check your type of drawing units.
5. Click on **Open** button. The file will be open as a component.

Note: When working with your own files check any known dimension with the Tape Measure tool. Resize your model if the size is incorrect. You might also need to open the Layers dialogue box and erase all layers that you brought from Autocad®. When you are prompted to move contents to a default layer, answer yes. Once all your entities are moved to

Layer 0, you can create another layer and move your Autocad® file group to it to free Layer 0 for Sketchup use. You might also want to lock the CAD layer to prevent erasing it unintentionally. Create scenes to toggle layer visibility.

6. Click on the **Zoom Extents** icon.
7. Select the **Top** view or Iso view.
8. Open **Styles** window and select Engineering style.
9. Start drawing on top of the floor plan. Use this example to practice of all the acquired concepts.

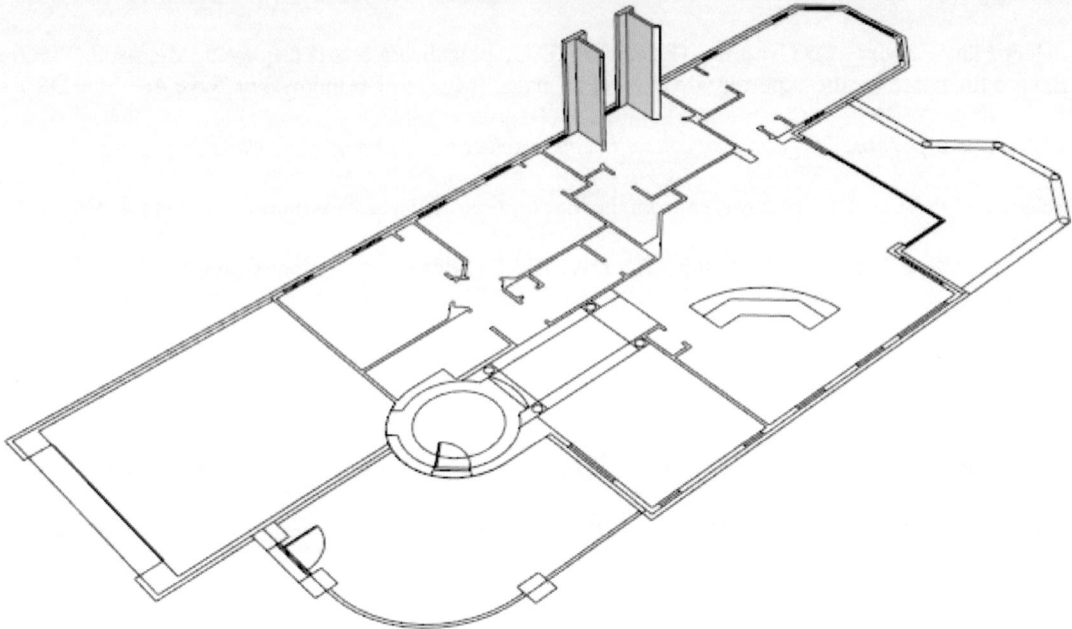

Note: It is strongly recommended that a CAD file be imported as a group instead of separate entities. If you import a file as a group you can use it as a reference and draw the required lines on top of the group. I found out that most people might have gaps in their files that can prevent faces creation. When you have existing geometry in your model the CAD file will be imported as a group. On the other hand if you are importing a CAD file when you do not have any existing geometry, all drawing lines and edges will be separate entities. You might need also to align axes to your CAD file before starting modeling with Sketchup.
To be able to develop some of the exercises you will need to download the resources file.

Feel free to contact me at sketchup-interior-design@nextcad.net to get access to those files or if you have any questions or any particular inquiries.

Final Exercise: Two-story apartment

Send an email to sketchup-interior-design@nextcad.net requesting this video.

Objectives
When you have completed this exercise you will be able to
- Understand how to organize a two-story project.
- Work on each room comfortably.

1. Create the first floor slab

1. Open a new file.
2. Draw a rectangle of 20'x30'.
3. Use the Push/Pull tool to give the slab 10" thickness.
4. Triple click on the slab with the Select tool active to select all the entities. Right-click/Make Group.
5. Open the Outliner / Rename the group as "First floor slab".

2. Create the first floor walls

1. Draw a new rectangle on top of the slab with the same dimensions.
2. Use the Offset tool and create an interior rectangle 4" from the edge.
3. Erase the inside face to avoid having two faces, one belonging to the slab and one belonging to the wall group.
4. Use the Push/Pull tool to create walls of 9' height.
5. Triple-click to select all the walls' entities with the Select tool active. Right-click/Make Group.
6. Open the Outliner / Rename the group "First floor walls".

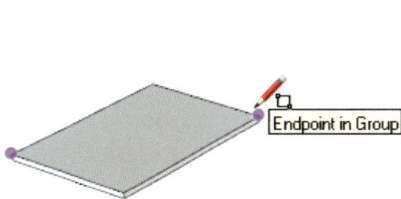
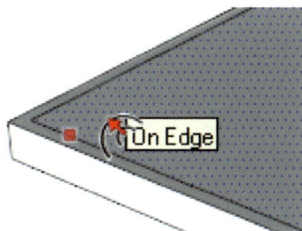
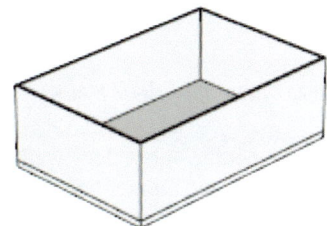

| (1) | (2) | (3)(4) |

3. Create the second floor slab

1. Select the First Floor Slab and copy it, placing it at the top edge of the walls.
2. Open the Outliner and rename it "Second floor slab".

Since this slab is going to cover only half the area of the first floor, you are going to make an opening for that part.

3. Double click on the "Second floor slab" to edit it and draw a line in the middle.
4. Select the Offset tool and create an interior offset at 4".
5. With the Pull/Push tool push inside the interior rectangle to the opposite edge to create a void. Close the group.

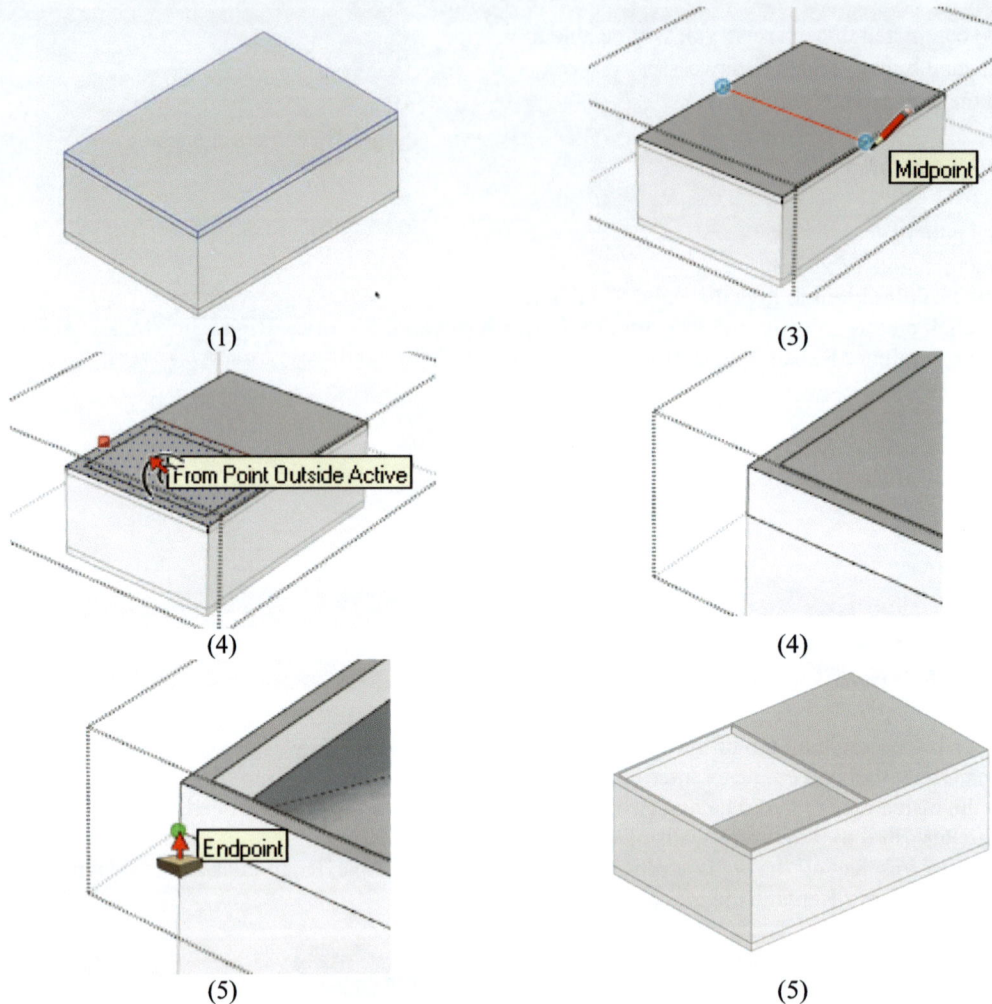

(1)

(3)

(4)

(4)

(5)

(5)

4. Create the second floor walls

1. Select the "First floor walls" and copy them on top of the "Second floor slab".
2. Open the Outliner and rename the group "Second floor walls"
3. Double-click on the "Second floor walls" group to enter to the edit mode.
4. Draw a rectangle on top of the "Second floor slab" to create a floor surface on the rooms' area.
5. Divide the right edge in 3 segments by selecting the edge, right-click / Divide.
6. Draw a line from the 1/3 endpoint to the opposite edge.
7. Draw a line from the midpoint of the top line to the bottom line.
8. Erase the left portion of the line; draw parallel lines to draw 4" interior walls.
9. Use the Pull/Push tool to build the interior walls as shown.
10. Erase the floor faces and leave only the interior and exterior walls.
11. Close group.

12. Save as Final_practice.

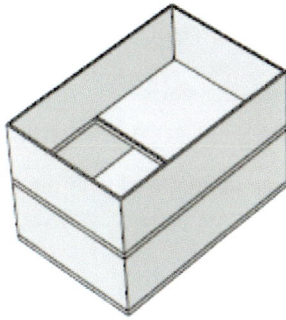

(1)

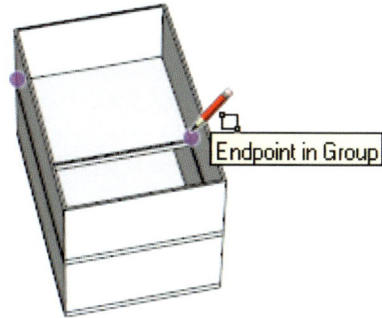

(4)

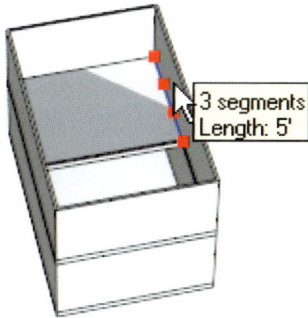

(5)

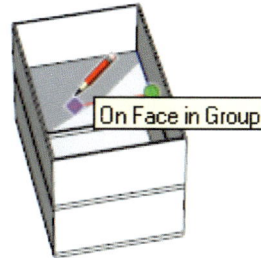

(6)

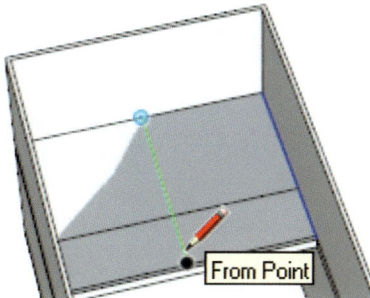

(7)(8)

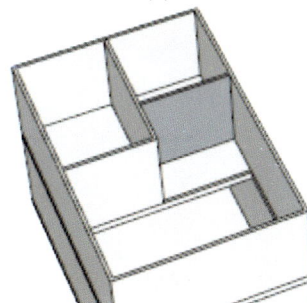

(9)

5. Create the stair

1. Open the Final_practice file.
2. Click on the "Second floor walls". Right-click / Hide.

You can apply your favorite method to create the stair. In this exercise we will combine the Divide method with the Push/Pull tool.

3. Draw a vertical line inferring with the blue axis as shown.
4. Select the line. Right-click / Divide until 15 segments tag appears. This number of segments will give you a rise of 7 7/8". Click.

5. Draw with the Line tool the first riser and tread. Start one level below the slab since the slab will serve as the last tread. Draw a 10" long line for the tread and a vertical line for the rise. Stop at the point that infers with the first endpoint of the line drawn in point 3.
6. Select the two last drawn lines and copy them to the endpoint of the rise vertical line.
7. Type 13x to reach the first floor level.
8. Hide the "First floor walls" and "First floor slab" to work easily with the stairs.
9. Draw the missing line at the floor level to complete the stair face.
10. Select the Push/Pull tool and make the stair 40" wide.
11. Unhide the first floor walls and push the last riser to create a landing up to the edge of the front wall.
12. Draw a 36" high railing.
13. Unhide the second floor walls and complete the railing.
14. Select with a crossing window all the stairs entities and create a group.
15. Open the Outliner and rename it "Stair".
16. Save.

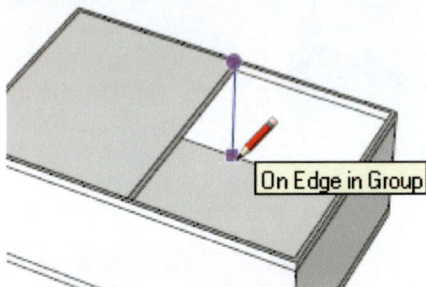

(3)

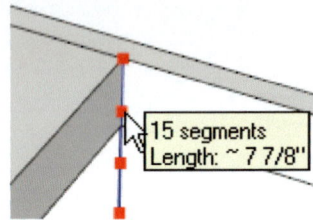

(4)

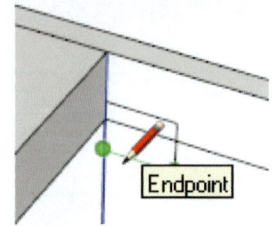

(5)

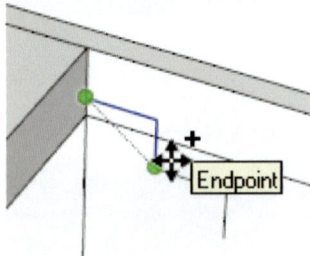

(6)

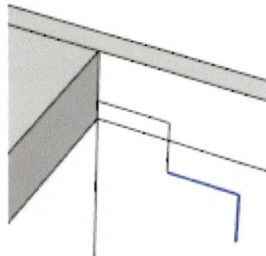

(6)

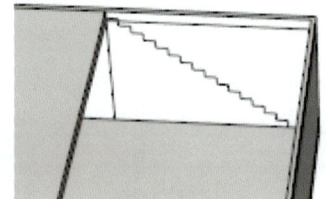

(7)

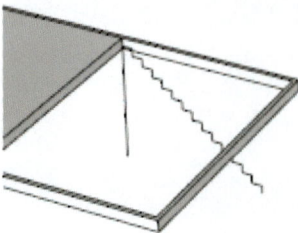

(8)

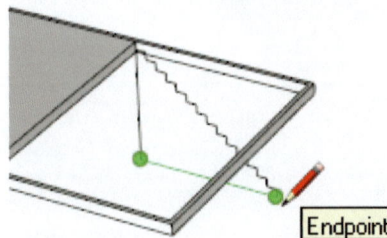

(9)

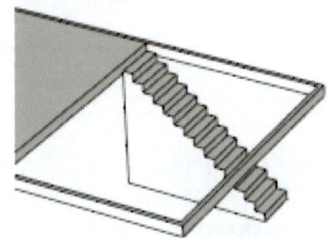

(10)

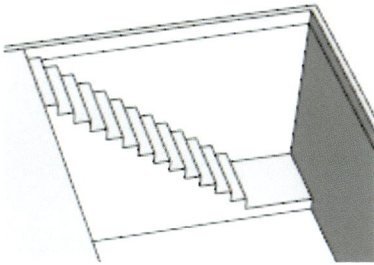

(11)

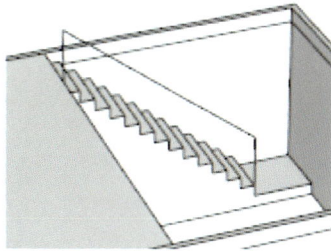

(12)

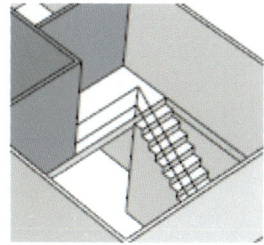

(13)

6. Insert windows and doors on the first and second floors. Complete interior walls on the first floor.

1. Open the Final_practice file.
2. Hide the second floor slab, second floor walls and stair groups.
3. Double-click to edit the first floor walls and insert windows. The pictures in this book have "Double-hung window 69 in. x 58 in. triple row with mullions" inserted.
4. Since you have two-face walls, you need to create openings on each window. Draw a rectangle in front of each window. Use the Push/Pull tool to reach the opposite side of the wall edge. Erase any face that is covering the inner or outer side of the window.
5. Unhide the stairwell and draw the interior walls. Erase the floor faces after drawing the walls.
6. Use Push/Pull to bring the walls to 9' height.
7. Insert interior and entry doors using components from the 3D Warehouse.

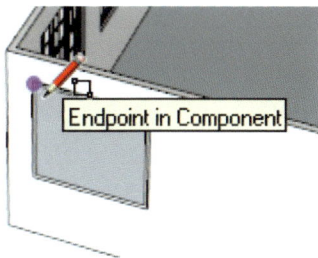

(4)

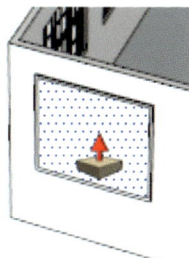

(4)

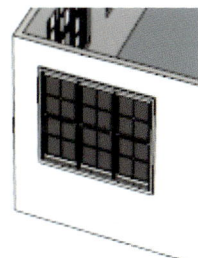

(4)

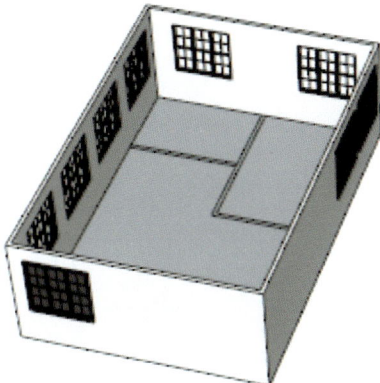

(5)

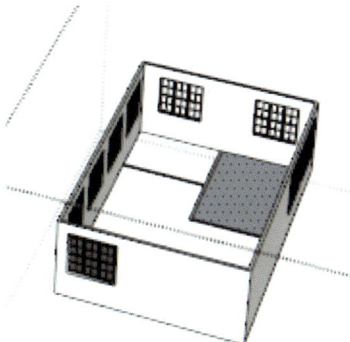

(5)

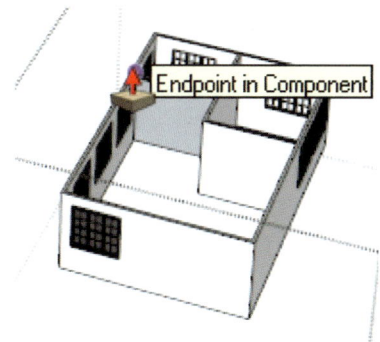

(6)

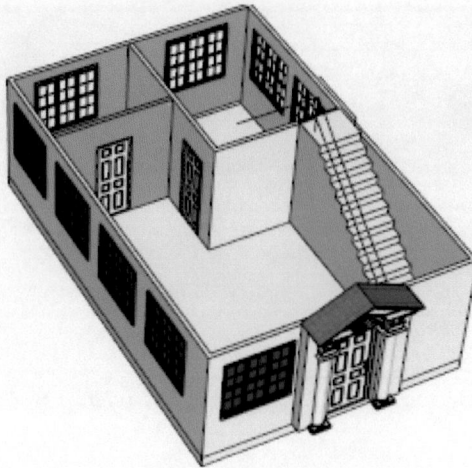

8. Hide all the entities that belong to the first floor and unhide the second floor walls.
9. Insert windows and doors, repeating steps to create the openings.

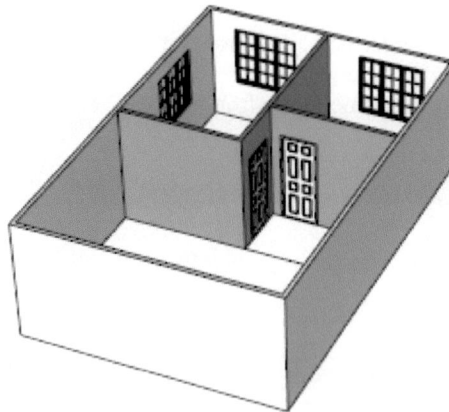

7. Create the ceiling and a roof

1. Unhide the first floor slab.
2. Copy it on top of the second floor walls.
3. Open the Outliner and rename it "roof".
4. Double-click on the roof group to enter to the edit mode.
5. Push all the edges out 12" and draw a line in the middle of the longest side.
6. Select that line and choose the Move tool. Move the line inferring with the blue axis.
7. Type 10'. Close group.

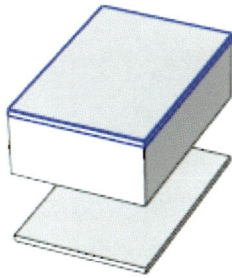

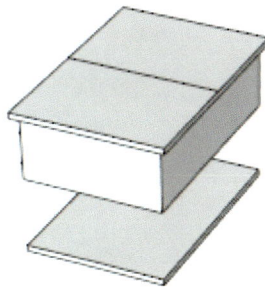

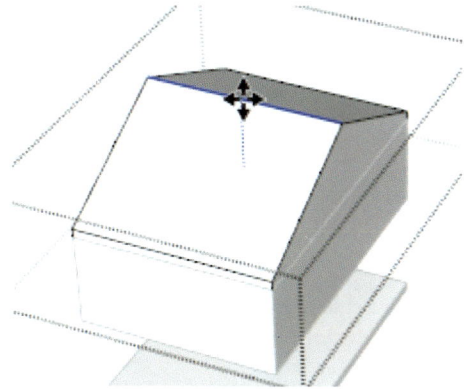

| (2) | (5) | (6) |

8. Use the Offset tool and the Push/Pull tool to create the trimming lines on both sides.
9. Unhide all the groups.

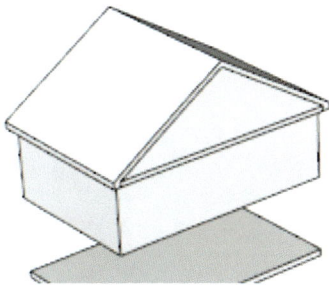

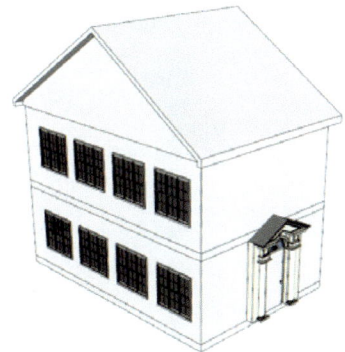

| (8) | (8) | (9) |

8. Reaching the inside with a section

1. Select the Section tool.
2. Place it on the left elevation. Click to make the section active.
3. Activate the Camera / Perspective option.
4. Choose the Position Camera tool and place it on the slab of the living room on the first floor.
5. Type 5'6" for the Eye Height.
6. Look around or walk around. You might need to disable the collision detection.
7. Open the Scenes dialog box and create a scene with a view that you like.
8. Save.

Note: Create scenes for every single view that you want to toggle to. Creating scenes for a first floor plan or second floor plan view, perspectives, sections, or furniture view will increase your productivity and the ability to reach any part of your model quickly.

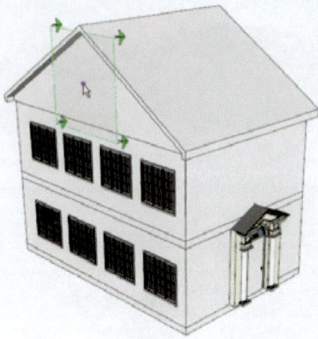 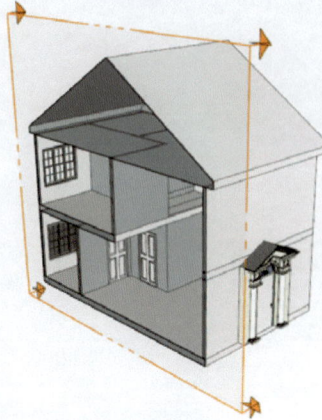 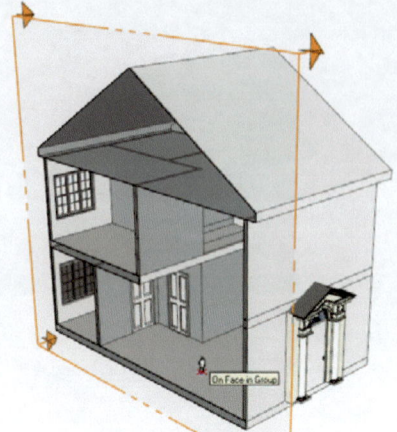

(2)   (2)   (3)

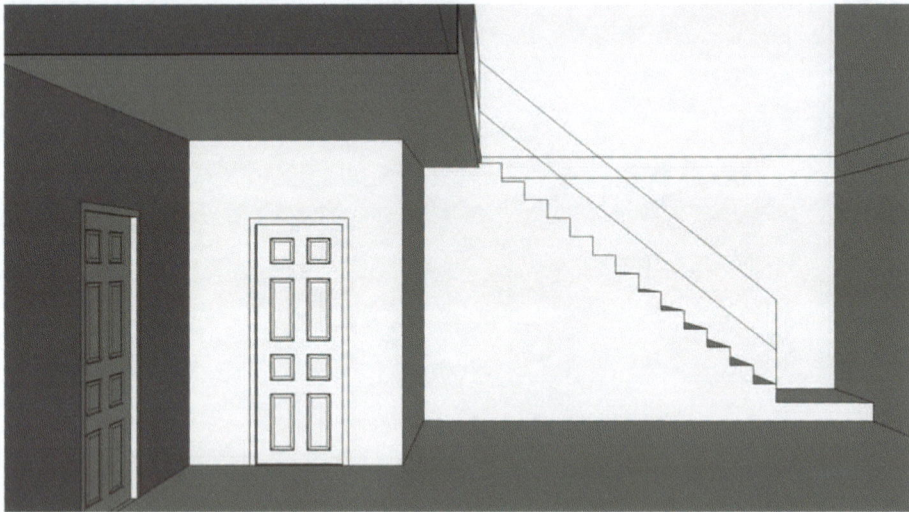

You can complete your model with furniture and create as many scenes that you want.

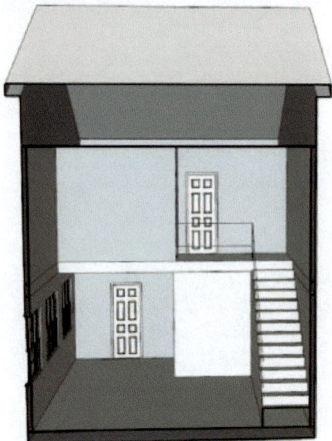 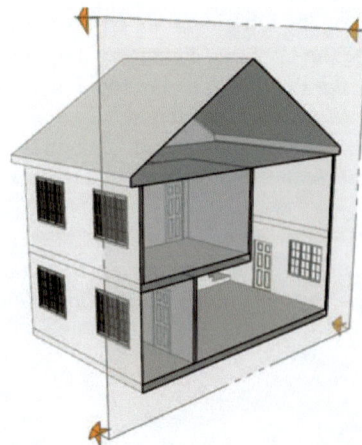

2340045R00032

Printed in Great Britain
by Amazon.co.uk, Ltd.,
Marston Gate.